Tuolumne Bouldering

The Best 20 Areas

by
Chris Summit

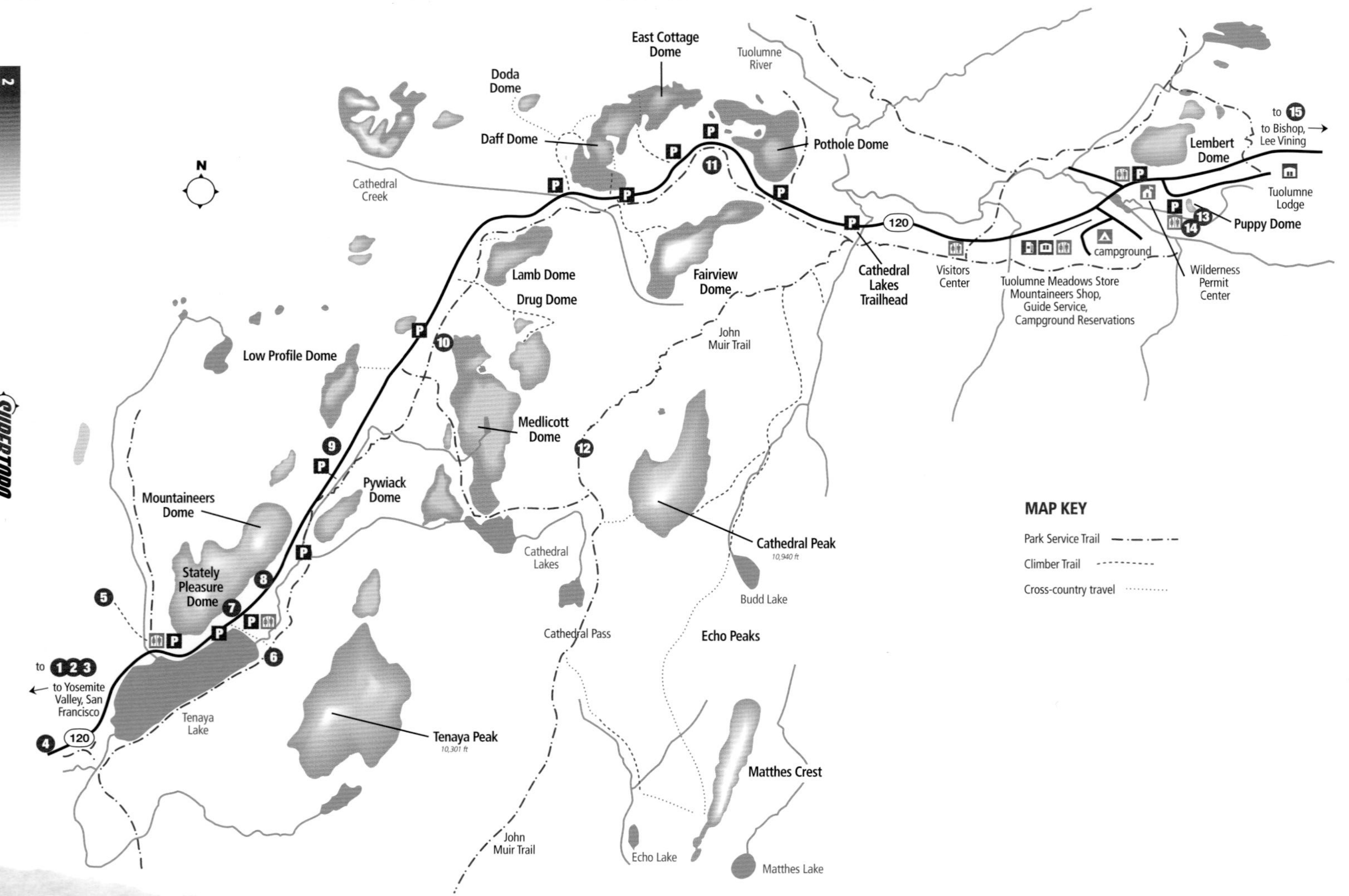

East Cottage Dome
Tuolumne River
Doda Dome
Daff Dome
Pothole Dome
to 15 to Bishop, Lee Vining
Lembert Dome
Tuolumne Lodge
Puppy Dome
13
14
N
Cathedral Creek
11
120
Lamb Dome
Fairview Dome
Drug Dome
Cathedral Lakes Trailhead
Visitors Center
Tuolumne Meadows Store
Mountaineers Shop,
Guide Service,
Campground Reservations
campground
Wilderness Permit Center
John Muir Trail
Low Profile Dome
10
Medlicott Dome
12
9
Pywiack Dome
Mountaineers Dome
MAP KEY
Park Service Trail
Climber Trail
Cross-country travel
Cathedral Peak
10,940 ft
Cathedral Lakes
Stately Pleasure Dome
8
7
5
Budd Lake
Cathedral Pass
Echo Peaks
6
to 1 2 3 to Yosemite Valley, San Francisco
Tenaya Lake
4
120
Tenaya Peak
10,301 ft
Matthes Crest
John Muir Trail
Echo Lake
Matthes Lake

Hetch Hetchy
Yosemite National Park
White Wolf
May Lake
Tuolumne Meadows
Tenaya Lake
Tamarack Flat
Yosemite Valley
Mono Lake
Lee Vining
to Reno
to Bishop
to CA-99, San Francisco
to CA-99, Merced
to CA-99, Fresno
120
140
41
167
395
N

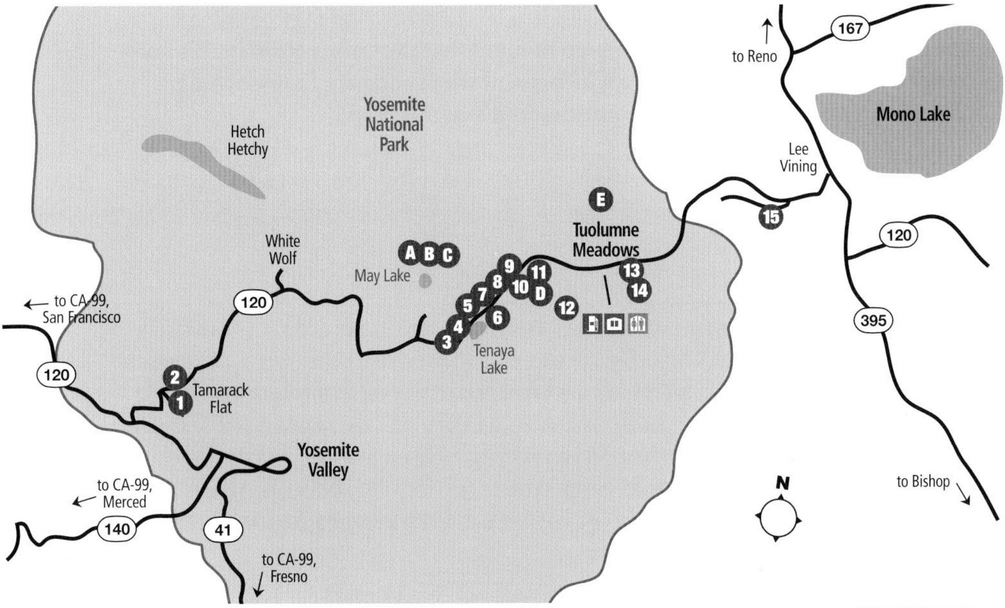

Warning

Climbing is an inherently dangerous sport in which severe injuries or death may occur. Relying on the information in this book may increase the danger.

When climbing you can only rely on your skill, training, experience, and conditioning. **If you have any doubts as to your ability to safely climb any route in this guide, do not try it.**

This book is neither a professional climbing instructor nor a substitute for one. **It is not an instructional book. Do not use it as one.** It contains information that is nothing more than a compilation of opinions about bouldering in Tuolumne. **These opinions are neither facts nor promises.** Treat the information as opinions and nothing more. Do not substitute these opinions for your own common sense and experience.

Assumption of Risk

There may be errors in this book resulting from the mistake of the authors and/or the people with whom they consulted. The information was gathered from a variety of sources, which may not have been independently verified. Those who provided the information may have made mistakes in their descriptions. The authors may have made mistakes in their conveyance of the information in this book. **The authors cannot, therefore, guarantee the correctness of any of the information contained in this book.** The topographical maps, photo-diagrams, difficulty ratings, protection ratings, approach and/or descent information, suggestions about equipment, and other matters may be incorrect or misleading. Fixed protection may be absent, unreliable, or misplaced. **You must keep in mind that the information in this book may be erroneous, so use your own judgement when choosing, approaching, climbing, or descending from a route described in this book.**

DO NOT USE THIS BOOK UNLESS YOU [AND YOUR ESTATE] PROMISE NEVER TO TRY TO SUE US IF YOU GET HURT OR KILLED.

Disclaimer of Warranties

THE AUTHORS AND PUBLISHER WARN THAT THIS BOOK CONTAINS ONLY THE AUTHORS' OPINIONS ON THE SUBJECTS DISCUSSED. THEY MAKE NO OTHER WARRANTIES, EXPRESSED OR IMPLIED, OF MERCHANTABILITY, FITNESS FOR PURPOSE, OR OTHERWISE, AND IN ANY EVENT, THEIR LIABILITY FOR BREACH OF ANY WARRANTY OR CONTRACT WITH RESPECT TO THE CONTENT OF THIS BOOK IS LIMITED TO THE PURCHASE PRICE OF THE BOOK. THEY FURTHER LIMIT TO SUCH PURCHASE PRICE THEIR LIABILITY ON ACCOUNT OF ANY KIND OF NEGLIGENT BEHAVIOR WHATSOEVER ON THEIR PART WITH RESPECT TO THE CONTENTS OF THIS BOOK.

Acknowledgements

Special thanks to these people for their help making the book:

John Bachar, Chris Falkenstein, Ron Kauk, the best mom in the world; Jeanie Anderson-Saludes and the best step dad; Bony Saludes, the best girlfriend; Valentine Cullen (imagealteration.com) and her beautiful and smart daughter; Holly Anne Grinnell, Chris McNamara (supertopo.com), Charlie Barrett, James Hosler (hoslerphotography.com), Marcos Nunez, Kenny Ariza, Jerry Dodrill (jerrydodrill.com), Randy Spurrier, David Safanda (safanda.com), and Steve McNamara.

Special thanks to these climbers for their help in the early development of bouldering in the Tuolumne area and for their first ascents (in no particular order):

John "Yabo" Yablonski
John Bachar
Bob Kamps
Dale Bard
Ron Kauk
Dave Yerian
Chris Falkenstein
Royal Robbins
Chris Vandiver
Tom Higgins
Vern Clevenger
Claude Fiddler
Lynn Hill
Charlie Barrett
Chris Sharma
Steve Schneider
Greg Loh
Chris Van Leuven
Marcos Nunez

and me and anyone else who did first ascents in the Tuolumne area. If I left someone out please let me know for the next edition.

- *Chris Summit*

Book Credits

Written by Chris Summit

Photos by Chris Summit, Chris Falkenstein, and John Bachar.

Edited by Steve McNamara, Chris McNamara

Layout by Chris McNamara

Printed in China on Forest Stewardship Council certified paper

Cover Photo: Ron Kauk on Texas Radio, V3 R. Photo: Chris Falkenstein

Table of Contents photo: Tuolumne Meadows at Sunset. Photo by Jerry Dodrill.

Back Cover: Chris Summit at May Lake. Photo: Summit Collection

Cover Design *by* David Safanda Design Solutions. www.safanda.com

This book is a testament to the years of dreaming, exploring, discovering and developing the rocks in Tuolumne and everywhere else on Planet Earth. More importantly, it is a testament to the years of our lives spent developing our minds, bodies and souls. Many thanks go out to the climbers who blaze the trails for us all, on and off the rocks and many thanks to all the people who helped with this book – life, at every level is a collaboration of sorts – there is no I in team. Let's all come together on this precious planet and help everyday, everyway to make it a better place for our futures - peace in peace out.

Chris Summit - Earth Day 2009

Introduction

By Chris Summit

Liv Sansov on Double Dyno at The Knobs. Photo by Chris Summit

High in the sky at over 8000 feet in elevation, Tuolumne is the largest sub-alpine meadow in the Sierras. When almost every other Sierra bouldering area is cooking in the heat of summer that is when The Meadows calls. Surrounded by stone, Tenaya Lake marks the western gate of the main Tuolumne climbing and bouldering areas and makes a perfect place to have a scenic picnic or take a dip on a hot summer day as well. The Tuolumne area is the ideal summertime boulder playground with perfect cool conditions to complement Bishop and Yosemite Valley's ripe fall, winter and spring bouldering seasons. Closed in winter, there is only a window of climb time each year for Tuolumne which equals about half the time you get at other areas with all year access. This shortened window of opportunity makes Tuolumne a place to be appreciated, cherished and respected each and every visit. With a rich bouldering history that reaches back to the roots of Yosemite climbing lore and first ascents by the original "Stonemasters," Tuolumne has always had a reputation for its unique knobs and challenging, uncharted and untamed rock in a wild alpine environment. Superb High Sierra granite with diorite knobs protruding from solid gold, white and black domes, cliffs, and boulders describes the rock. Thin and slabby, run-out face climbs on huge granite domes describes most of the routes. The bouldering is often very similar, just condensed into a shorter, more intense but equally hair-raising experience. In the end, of course, it's always a very rewarding, satisfying and memorable experience. Head-spinning highballs, splitter cracks, balance slabs, thin and tenuous knob pinching face climbs, and epic long traverses describes the majority of boulder styles. A few overhanging problems are in the Tuolumne area but they are not the norm. The steep stuff is, however, excellent and on mostly well-featured, solid stone with burly, powerful moves mixed with the classic technical granite moves and quite often a heinous mantel top out. Bouldering in Tuolumne is an experience not to be missed.

SuperTopo.com

The information below is available at supertopo.com with links directly to the sources for easier trip planning.

Essential Tuolumne Beta

Below is some fundamental information for planning a trip to Tuolumne. However, for more updated and extensive information you should visit the Tuolumne Beta Page on the SuperTopo web site: www.supertopo.com/climbingareas/tuolumne.html

Getting There

Tuolumne Meadows is located 1.5 hours northeast of Yosemite Valley. Since most climbers start their trip to Tuolumne by first driving through or near Yosemite Valley, you should visit the SuperTopo Yosemite Beta Page at www.supertopo.com/climbingareas/yosemite.html. There you will find more information and links for airports, buses, trains, and car travel.

Air Travel

Reno/Tahoe Airport is the closest airport to Tuolumne. From there, you will need to rent a car (three-hour drive) or take a bus or shuttle to Mammoth. The bus service is The Crest/Inyo-Mono Transit (800-922-1930), and the shuttles are the Mammoth Shuttle (760-934-6588) or Sierra Express (760-937-8294). From Mammoth take YARTS to Tuolumne (see Bus travel). Oakland or San Francisco airports are farther from Tuolumne but are preferred over Reno/Tahoe because there are more flights to choose from. You can also fly into Sacramento or Fresno. Each of these places is a 3.5- to 5-hour drive from Tuolumne Meadows.

Bus Travel

YARTS (877-989-2787; www.yarts.com) provides bus transportation from Yosemite Valley to Tuolumne and from the Eastern Sierra to Tuolumne. During July through Labor Day, YARTS leaves from the Tuolumne Meadows Store every morning and from Yosemite Lodge each evening. It provides access between Yosemite and Mammoth, with the schedule and prices varying according to demand, even depending on day. Once in Tuolumne, a free shuttle bus provides convenient access throughout the Tuolumne Meadows area between the Tuolumne Lodge and Olmsted Point (including Tenaya Lake) during the middle part of the summer, and even sometimes to Tioga Pass a few times a day.

Car Travel

From Yosemite Valley, it's a 1.5-hour drive east on Highway 120 to Tuolumne Meadows. It's a 4.5-hour drive to Tuolumne from the Bay Area, a 3-hour drive from the Tahoe area, and about a 1.5-hour drive from Bishop.

Gas is available by next to the Tuolumne Meadows Store, 15 miles east in Lee Vining, and on Highway 120 at Crane Flat.

If you don't have a car, you can rent one at any airport or major city. International climbers who stay in the United States for more than a month often buy a cheap used car in San Francisco or Los Angeles and sell it (or scrap it) at the end of their trip.

Driving times and distances to Tuolumne

From	Time (hours)	Distance (miles)
Boulder, CO	18:00	1,150
Fresno, CA	3:30	150
Truckee, CA	3:00	150
Los Angeles, CA	6:00	340
Mammoth, CA	1:00	50
Oakland, CA	4:30	220
Sacramento, CA	4:00	210
Salt Lake City, UT	10:00	620
San Francisco, CA	4:30	230
Yosemite Valley	1:30	60

When to Climb

Tuolumne Meadows has some of the best weather of any alpine rock climbing area on Earth. That said, Tuolumne is in a massive mountain range that receives severe thunderstorms, lightning, and rare major Pacific weather systems throughout the summer.

All climbing in Tuolumne is accessible from Highway 120. Because of its high elevation, Highway 120 east of Crane Flat and west of Lee Vining is closed in the winter. The road closes on the first snow of the year (usually November) and opens sometime in late May to June, depending on the snow year. During the winter, it is possible to climb in Tuolumne, but few people make the arduous ski in.

During early season (late May–June depending on snow year), Tuolumne conditions are often the best: no crowds, no mosquitoes, and long days. However, some approaches and climbs may be wet or snowy. Around June 15 the crowds arrive in Tuolumne—along with the mosquitoes. The crowds are not bad relative to Yosemite, but you will probably have to wait in line for the most classic routes. The mosquitoes on the other hand, can be terrible. Be sure to bring long pants, long sleeve shirts, and bug repellent. In September, the crowds and mosquitoes leave Tuolumne and while the climbing conditions are still great, the days become short and the nights frigid.

Thunderstorm cycles are common in the summer. Typically, the storms hit in mid-afternoon and slowly increase in strength over several days, clearing up each night. However, heavy thunderstorms and rain can set in for days at a time. And in a few recent summers, an almost total lack of thunderstorms over the entire summer have perplexed locals.

Current Road and Weather

There is no specific weather phone report for Tuolumne so your best bet is to check the general High Sierra weather at www.supertopo.com. For current road conditions, call 209-372-0200, or the CalTrans voice-activated system for major highway conditions at 800-gas-road or 916-445-7623

Staying in Tuolumne

Unlike the Yosemite Valley experience, Tuolumne Meadows is relatively uncrowded and serene and provides just enough basic services to comfortably camp. If you are craving some better food, more services, or just a day excursion, Lee Vining, Mono Lake, and Mammoth Lakes are all less than an hour away.

Camping

The only campground in Tuolumne is the Tuolumne Meadows Campground, which is centrally located and very large (over 300 sites). Half of the sites can be reserved in advance at www.recreation.gov (reserve them at least 2-3 months in advance for peak times) and half of the sites are on a first come, first served basis (stand in line in early morning to ensure you get a site.) Sites cost $20 per night with a six-person, two-car limit. Be aware that mosquitoes can be particularly fierce and bears patrol the campground so proper food storage is mandatory.

Located 7 to 12 miles east from Tuolumne Meadows are ten Forest Service campgrounds, many of which are first come, first served. Several of these campgrounds are at elevations higher than Tuolumne Meadows and can help with acclimation. Twelve miles east of Tuolumne Meadows, the campgrounds in lower Lee Vining Canyon are lower altitude, more sheltered from the wind, and near to services in Lee Vining. You will pay between $12 and $17 per night on a first come, first served basis. The prices at these campgrounds have climbed steeply in recent years, in some cases more than doubling in less than a decade.

Along Highway 120 toward Yosemite Valley are several additional campgrounds with moderate to long drives (30 minutes to one hour). The campground reservation office in Tuolumne has information on current campground conditions.

Lodges and Cabins

In addition to campsites, there are more plush accommodations available in Tuolumne and the High Sierra, including the Tuolumne Meadows Lodge, White Wolf, and the High Sierra Camps (www.yosemitepark.com/html/accommodation.html). Just outside of the park boundary is the Tioga Pass Resort (www.tiogapassresort.com), which offers cabins year-round, a small restaurant, and an espresso bar. Drive 15 miles east from Tuolumne Meadows and you will reach Lee Vining, a small town with a few motels, restaurants, and other basic services.

Food

A limited selection of high-priced groceries are available at the Tuolumne Meadows store. In addition, you can purchase groceries in Lee Vining at the Lee Vining Market. Mammoth has a large Vons supermarket.

The Tuolumne Meadows Grill serves hamburgers, fries, etc, but has very limited hours, closing hours before dark in mid-summer. The Tuolumne Lodge has a restaurant that serves breakfast and dinner in the midde part of summer. Eight miles east of Tuolumne Meadows, the Tioga Pass Resort houses a cozy dining room with good food. Surprisingly, the Mobil Gas Station, located 14 miles from Tuolumne Meadows in Lee Vining, has the best food in the area. This isn't just any gas station—Tioga Toomey's Whoa Nellie Deli has a great selection of sandwiches, pizzas, fish tacos, and a variety of other savory treats for breakfast, lunch, and dinner. Frequent local bands and even a trapeze out front are other features of this unusual gas station.

Climbing Gear and Climbing Guides

The Tuolumne Mountain Shop (209-372-8436) located at the Tuolumne gas station offers a small selection of climbing equipment. For a more extensive selection of gear, you will need to drive 50 miles to Mammoth (Mammoth Mountaineering Supply; (888-395-3951, www.mammothgear.com), 90 miles to Bishop (Wilson's Eastside Sports; 760-873-7520, www.eastsidesports.com), or 60 miles back to Yosemite Valley (Yosemite Mountain Shop; 209-372-8396, www.yosemitegifts.com/wetoyomosh.html).

You can get climbing instruction and arrange for a guide through the Yosemite Mountaineering School (209-372-8344), which is based in Tuolumne at the Mountain Shop/gas station.

Altitude

At elevation it takes a few days for most people to adjust to the rarefied air, so drink plenty of water and take it easy. On your first day in Tuolumne, climb a route with a short approach to let yourself acclimate. In addition, eat a low-fat diet for the first day or two. Wear extra sunscreen and a hat—the UV levels are greater at altitude and severe sunburns can happen quickly.

Thunderstorms and Lightning

Tuolumne has mostly beautiful, sunny weather in the summer, yet severe thunderstorms occur. Small, puffy clouds seen before 10 a.m. are a frequent predictor of afternoon rain, hail and, worst of all, lightning. Thunderstorms often appear in cycles and generally during periods of hot, calm weather in the Central Valley.

Lightning tends to hit high points, trees, and water, but will also hit low points next to high rocks, flat areas near trees, and dry land around lakes. A climber was struck by lightning on Cathedral Peak in 2000, and many other close calls have occurred.

Know how to perform CPR. Unlike nearly any other type of injury that stops the heart, electrical shock victims can suddenly awaken even after extended CPR. But remember, the best strategy is to avoid thunderstorms in the first place. If you're on a climb and get nervous about developing clouds, it's time to turn around.

Bears, Marmots, and Mosquitoes

Bears have damaged cars for as little as a stick of gum or an empty soda can. If you want what's yours to remain yours, remember three things: bears are hungry, smart, and strong.

When bears smell food, even if it's locked in your trunk or glove compartment, they shift into high gear. They get turned on by odors of containers that used to contain food. They even go for toothpaste and sunscreen. Bears don't need to smell food; they see something like a grocery bag or an ice chest, and associate it with food. In fact, they don't even need to see that much. If a bear sees clutter inside a car, he'll think, "I wonder what's under all that stuff?" and go to work.

Breaking into a car is a trivial exercise for a bear. He inserts his claws at the top of the door frame and pulls down. Then he climbs in and trashes the car. You can't outsmart or outmuscle a bear. Always stash your food in one of the bear-proof storage lockers provided by the Park Service in the campground, at various trailheads including Cathedral Lakes, or at the Wilderness Permit Center.

If camping in the backcountry, use bear canisters, which are available at the Wilderness Permit Center. Tuolumne bears are experienced at cutting the lines to hung food, and the tattered remnants of the lines can be observed on nearly any tree near a backcountry campsite.

In addition to bears, be on the lookout for marmots. Cute from a distance, these plump critters love nothing more than scrounging for food in climbing packs while you watch helplessly from two pitches up. Be sure to hang your backpack high on a tree branch—even if it does not have food in it. Marmots are tough, smart, and strong-toothed and can quickly gnaw through nearly anything—leave zippers open.

Nasty mosquitoes are very common for most of the summer in Tuolumne, so come prepared. Consider long sleeve pants and shirts, which not only help with mosquitoes but help prevent sunburns.

Cell Phones, Wireless Internet, misc. Stuff

The closest wireless internet to Tuolumne is Latte Da coffee shop in Lee Vining (you need your own laptop). Cell phones work sporadically through Tuolumne if you have ATT. Other carriers are less reliable. There is a good signal around the Tuolumne Store and on top of most domes.

Miscellaneous Beta

Showers cost $2 and are available at the Tuolumne Meadows lodge between noon and 3 p.m. There is a post office located next to the Tuolumne Store, which is open most of the season.

A message board is located outside the Tuolumne Meadows Store, and another larger one is along the entrance road to the campground. Most climbers use the Store board, but make sure if arranging messages with friends to specify which board.

The Tuolumne Meadows Stables (209-372-8348) is the pack station in Tuolumne.

The nearest ATM is at the Lee Vining Market. The nearest bank is Mammoth. You can get cash back with a credit card purchase from the Tuolumne Store.

Ron Kauk on The Cross at The Knobs. Photo by Chris Falkenstein

Ron Kauk at The Knobs. Photo from John Bachar.

Knobs

By John Bachar

Back in the late seventies, I had heard stories of climbing the magnificent domes of Tuolumne. Bob Kamps and Royal Robbins were putting up wicked run out edging routes. Little did I know but there was some seriously great bouldering to be done.

We didn't have vertical or overhanging face climbing at the time so our only way to get that fix was by bouldering. We had no idea there existed any steep bouldering potential in the Meadows. Everybody thought the Valley was where it was all happening until Dale Bard started climbing there in the summers. He came back with stories of what we wanted to hear, "There are some killer boulders up there man." We listened to his tales of fine granite blocks with "crystals" on overhanging blank faces.

Since we didn't have cars we finally made it up a few days later. The car stopped when we first saw the Cube. Then we hit the Knobs. It was all new. Pristine, unclimbed problems were everywhere.

There were already a lot of Bob Kamps' problems around and Dale Bard was putting up some testpieces as well. Texas Radio and Machine World were some of his best. In the late seventies and early eighties Ron Kauk, Chris Falkenstein, Ed Barry, myself, and others had put up more stuff. By mid eighties, sport climbing had hit the States, which allowed me to have the place virtually to myself. People just weren't into bouldering anymore, so by pure luck I had the good fortune of "discovering" the Gunks and bagging all the first ascents.

Still, the majesty of the granite and the depth of the blue skies draw, to this day, climbers and boulderers from all over the world. Unclimbed gemstones are awaiting discovery by present and future dreamers. Regardless of the times or the fashions, the Meadows holds a mystique and a rich tradition which will never leave us. It will continue to inspire us all at our deepest levels.

See you at the boulders.

Spirit of The Meadows

By Ron Kauk

The summer of 1972 I found myself learning how to stand in aid slings at Puppy Dome. I'd signed up for a week-long Yosemite Mountaineering School course; I think they called it Alpine Craft. At 14 years old this was like living a dream. My guides were TM Herbert – with his white t-shirt and cotton knickers he was the real thing – a true Yosemite climber; Chris Vandiver took us up on the Great White Book (5.6) in his Levis, styli shirt and longer hair; Loyd Price showed us how to make technical free moves at the Knobs bouldering area before it was the Knobs bouldering area. To finish the week my brother and I hiked to the top of Mount Lyell. It has been 36 summers since then in Tuolumne Meadows for me. Every summer has brought new adventures, education and more understanding about how precious and beautiful these boulders and domes are. Tuolumne continues to teach me about what it means to feel a sense of place and how important it is for us to respect nature.

As a climbing community we have been given a great privilege to climb in Tuolumne Meadows. It will be up to us all to take good care of the areas we climb at so Let's move into the future together and enjoy the opportunity and freedom to become better climbers and human beings.

Tamarack Boulders

Number of problems: **35 total/ 20 listed**

Time of Day: **Sun/Shade Mix**

Difficulty: **VB-V6/7**

Coming from the west, these roadside boulders are the first you come to on CA-120. Most are found on Tamarack Flat Road and are only worth a stop if you just can't wait any longer, you're camping at the secluded Tamarack Flat Campground or it's raining or snowing up in the Tuolumne Meadows area. Not that there aren't a fair amount of problems here, but compared to how many are just 45 minutes away to the east around the Meadows it is just a pit stop.

The rocks are also not as knobby as the Meadows, having more edges, buckets, cracks, and arêtes. There are also a few good problems in the campground at the bottom of the road and potential for more all over the Tamarack area.

Marcos Nunez flashes Tamarack Dyno (V2).

Driving directions

About four miles east of Crane Flat. About 55 miles west of Lee Vining/CA-395 (about 35 miles west of the Tuolumne Meadows Store) on Tioga Pass Rd./CA-120 near Tamarack Flat. Follow separate directions to the individual areas:

TAMARACK ROAD BOULDERS

Tamarack Road Boulders

3.8 miles east of Crane Flat and about 54.5 miles west of Lee Vining/CA395 on Tioga Pass Rd./CA-120 turn onto Tamarack Flat Rd. and drive downhill toward the campground for 0.2 miles and park on the left next to the main boulders or on the right at 0.3 miles from Tioga Pass Rd./ CA-120. Parking GPS 37.76200, -119.77066

Approach

No approach. The boulders are alongside the road or within a stone's throw.

Number of problems by difficulty

VB	V0	V1	V2	V3	V4	V5	V6	V7	V8	V9	V10	≥V11
1	3	6	4	0	1	0	1	0	0	0	0	0

North Boulders

❑ **1. V2/3★★** Short crack.

❑ **2. VB★★** Left side of slab with jug crack ledges or VB Jug arête on right side of slab.

❑ **3. V1★★** Bulge face..

South Boulder

❑ **4. V1★★** Flake to slab top.

❑ **5. V0★★★** Slab to hueco top – easy way to up/downclimb.

❑ **6. V1/2★★** Left-hand undercling start to slope jug to top.

❑ **7. V2/3★★** Right-hand undercling, go up left past slope jug to top.

Dyno Boulder

❑ **8. V1★★** Stand start on diagonal crimper edges go up over short bulge.

❑ **9. V?** Steep slashed bulge/face.

❑ **10. V2/3★★** Stand start in dirty scoop go over short bulge left of "Tamarack Dyno."

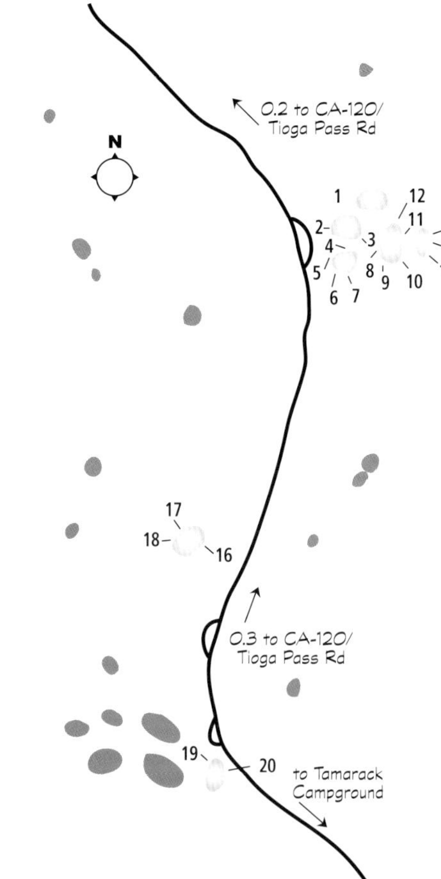

❏ **11. Tamarack Dyno V2★★★** Stand start dyno from big jug to little jug – V3 Sit start.

11a. V4 Low right start same as (V6/7) right arête low start.

❏ **12. V6/7★★★** Low start overhanging right arête – V5 Stand start.

Green Face

❏ **13. V0★★** Diagonal crack up left side of face.

❏ **14. V?★★** Center slab face.

❏ **15. V1★★** Right slab face.

Dirty Hueco Boulder

❏ **16. V!?** Steep bulge facing road.

❏ **17. V?** Center of face on the back hillside to dirty hueco?

❏ **18. V?** Right face on back hillside past hollow pockets to dirty hueco?

Hueco Mantel Boulder

❏ **19. Hueco Mantel V0★★★** Stand start tips layback dihedral up to hueco/thread mantel. (up/downclimb) – V1 Sit start.

❏ **20. V1/2★★** Slab facing road.

The Roadside Classic; Hueco Mantel (V0)

Tamarack North/East

Number of problems: **10 total/5 listed**

Time of Day: **Sun/Shade Mix - South Facing**

Difficulty: **V0–V4**

A few okay boulders with a few okay problems are across CA-120 to the north of Tamarack Flat Rd. and stretch about two more miles to the east of Tamarack Flat Rd. along both sides of CA-120. There is some potential for new problems and even to find some new boulders. Keep an eye out; they could be just out of sight.

Tamarack North

Across CA-120 from Tamarack Flat Rd. intersection and stretching a few miles down the north side of CA-120 all the way to about Tamarack East are a few boulders with some problems and some potential for more – None Are Listed.

Tamarack East

About 6.2 miles east of Crane Flat | About 52 miles west of Lee Vining/CA-395.

Parking Area/Trailhead: Park next to the boulders in a big, obvious, dirt turnout with a nice view on the south side of Tioga Pass Rd./CA-120.

Approach

No approach — the boulders are a spit from the car parked alongside the road.

Scruncher, Tamarack East.

Tamarack Crack (west to east)

❑ **1. V?** Steep wall facing away from road.

❑ **2. V?** Traverse?

❑ **3. Tamarack Smack V2★★** Stand start horizontal, smack sloper, top out! V2/3 Sit.

❑ **4. Tamarack Crack V0★★** Splitter jam crack to flat lip - V1/2 Left traverse start.

❑ **5. Scruncher V4★★** Sit start incut diagonal crack go up into V1 Stand start.

Number of problems by difficulty

VB	V0	V1	V2	V3	V4	V5	V6	V7	V8	V9	V10	≥V11
0	1	0	1	0	1	0	0	0	0	0	0	0

3
4
5
1

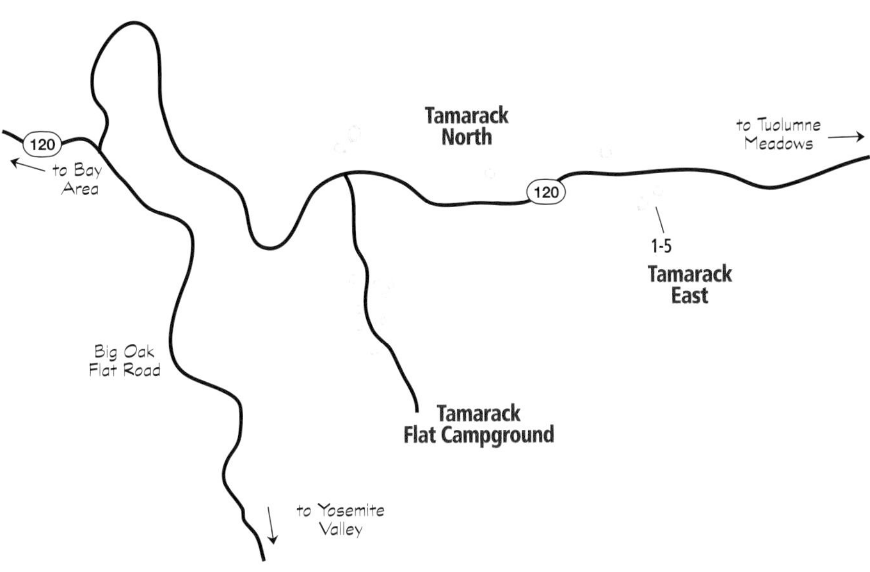

120
to Bay Area
Tamarack North
120
to Tuolumne Meadows
1-5
Tamarack East
Big Oak Flat Road
Tamarack Flat Campground
to Yosemite Valley

Olmstead Boulders

Number of problems: **25 total/12 listed**

Time of Day: **Sun/Shade Mix**

Difficulty: **V0-V8**

The views of Half Dome at sunset from the popular tourist pull-off at the point are unforgettable. Below the rocky viewpoint is a big boulder with a couple of highball splitter cracks known as the Olmstead Cracks (V0-V1). On the opposite side of CA-120, just a bit west, is a big pond/lagoon with a few good problems scattered around it and potential for maybe a few more. On the backside of the pond/lagoon is the classic of the Olmstead area: the highball Conquistador V8.

Summit does Olmstead Crack, circa 1990's
Photo Sean Brady.

DIRECTIONS:

Olmstead Canyon
28.60 miles east of Crane Flat (0.3 miles west of Olmstead Point) + 29.80 miles west of Lee Vining/CA-395 (about 10.8 miles west of the Tuolumne Meadows Store) on Tioga Pass Rd./CA-120.

Olmstead Boulders (Olmstead Canyon)
Parking GPS: 37.81253, -119.48933

APPROACH:

From the paved pullout on the north side of Tioga Pass Rd. (CA-120), follow a trail to the northwest past some boulders on the right to The Roof Boulder in the forest about a one-to-two-minute hike from the road. Another one-to-two-minute hike further northwest past a small lagoon/pond on the left will get you to Conquistador.

Boulder #1 + #2

❏ **1. V4/5★★** Stand start arête?

❏ **2. V5/6★★** Sit start short overhang to sloper lip top out?

❏ **3. VB★★** Slab arêtes.

The Roof (R to L)

❏ **4. The Roof V4★★★** Sit start short, steep roof.

❏ **5. The Offwidth V!?** Offwidth!

❏ **6. V3** Sit start left roof?

❏ **7. V?**

Number of problems by difficulty

VB	V0	V1	V2	V3	V4	V5	V6	V7	V8	V9	V10	≥V11
0	2	1	0	1	1	1	0	0	1	0	0	0

Conquistador Boulder

❑ **8. Conquistador V8★★★★** High and clean, mega classic! FA: Some Spanish guys - 90s

❑ **9. V?**

Lagoon Rock

❑ **10. Creature of the Black Lagoon V0R★★★** Traverse into highball crack over lagoon/ pond.

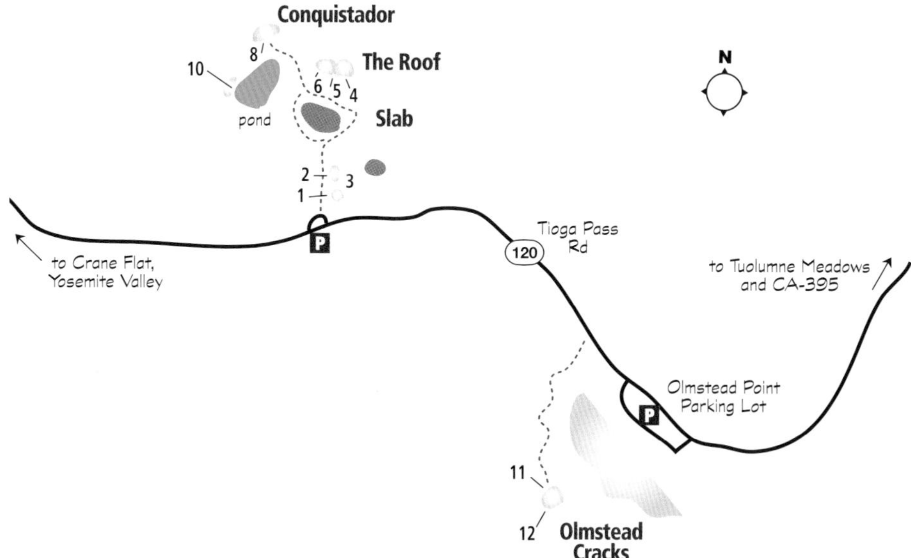

Olmstead Point

28.90 miles east of Crane Flat (big paved parking lot/viewpoint of Half Dome!) + 29.50 miles west of Lee Vining/CA-395 (about 10.5 miles west of the Tuolumne Meadows Store) on Tioga Pass Rd./CA-120

Olmstead Boulders (Olmstead Point) Parking GPS: 37.81098, -119.48603

APPROACH:

From the west end of the huge Olmstead Point Parking Lot, hike downhill to the west and then back south. Below the main cliff-band with the tourist viewpoint on top is a boulder with a couple of splitter semi-highball boulder cracks.

Olmstead Cracks

❑ **11. Olmstead Crack V1★★★★** Semi highball, vertical splitter jam crack!

❑ **12. V0R★★** Crack on back - easiest way up/down.

Rick's Boulder (The Procrastinator)

Number of problems: **5 total/2 listed**

Time of Day: **Shady All Day - East Facing**

Difficulty: **V5R**

Now this is a highball! Or is it a solo? If you're not sure, then it's a top rope. Either way it's a classic. This nearly roadside clifflet is about 35 feet tall with a tall diagonal crack splitting its main face. A few more problems are found here.

DIRECTIONS:

30.20 miles east of Crane Flat + 28.20 miles west of Lee Vining/CA-395 (1.1 miles west of Murphy Creek on the northwest side of Tioga Pass Rd./CA-120). Parking GPS: 37.82465, -119.47518

APPROACH:

The obvious 30-foot wall with a diagonal crack splitting its main face. Visible from the parking alongside Tioga Pass Rd. (CA-120) no more than a one-minute walk.

❑ **1. The Procrastinator V5R★★★** Diagonal rail/crack - highball/solo or top rope.!?

❑ **2. V?** Traverse.

Ridgetop Boulders

Number of problems: **25 total/15 listed**

Time of Day: **Sun/Shade Mix All Day**

Difficulty: **VB-V9**

On top of the prominent ridge between the May Lake area and Tenaya Lake area, these boulders have awesome views on almost every side. The classic nicknamed "The Booze Bottle" (V6/V9 sit) after its bottle shape is a steep face and arête challenge. There are also plenty of other good problems from VB to V-hard all around the big boulders that sport The Booze Bottle and potential for more.

DIRECTIONS:

31.20 miles east of Crane Flat (about 2.4 miles east of Olmstead Point) + 27.20 miles west of Lee Vining/CA-395 (about 7.7 miles west of the Tuolumne Meadows Store) on Tioga Pass Rd./CA-120.

Ridgetop Boulders/Murphy Creek Parking GPS: 37.83405, -119.46335

Ridgetop Boulders GPS 37.83871, -119.47311

APPROACH:

From the Murphy Creek Trailhead Parking Lot, walk across Tioga Pass Rd. (CA-120) toward the boulder alongside the road next to the creek just left of the trailhead. The side of the boulder that faces the road has the Murphy Crack (V2/3). From the boulder cross Murphy Creek and hike west (uphill) straight toward the ridge, passing a small pond about three-quarters of the way up. The boulders are on top of the ridge.

Andrew Zaslove does the #4 (V0) crack

Murphy Creek Boulder

Next to the road and creek at the base of the trail to the Ridgetop.

❑ **1. Murphy Crack V2/3★** Stand start diagonal splitter crack with dirty top out.

Ridgetop Boulder

❑ **2. V0★★** Slab face.

❑ **3. V1★** Traverse shelf left into slab arête/face.

Split Boulder

❑ **4. V0★★** Right-hand layback crack.

❑ **5. V3★★** Stand start off high right-hand edge and go up.

Number of problems by difficulty

VB	V0	V1	V2	V3	V4	V5	V6	V7	V8	V9	V10	≥V11
0	2	3	2	3	1	2	1	0	1	1	0	0

❑ **6. V1★★** Sit start on horizontal rail and go up over sloper lip on short face - Downclimb

❑ **7. V3★★** Stand start left arête/crack between trees - V4 Sit start jam crack up into stand.

Booze Bottle

❑ **8. V4R!★★★** Stand start left-hand layback to sloper highball top out!? Classic!? FA John Bachar.

❑ **9. V5★★★** Stand start left of Booze Bottle on gold patina edges and go up right to top out. FA John Bachar.

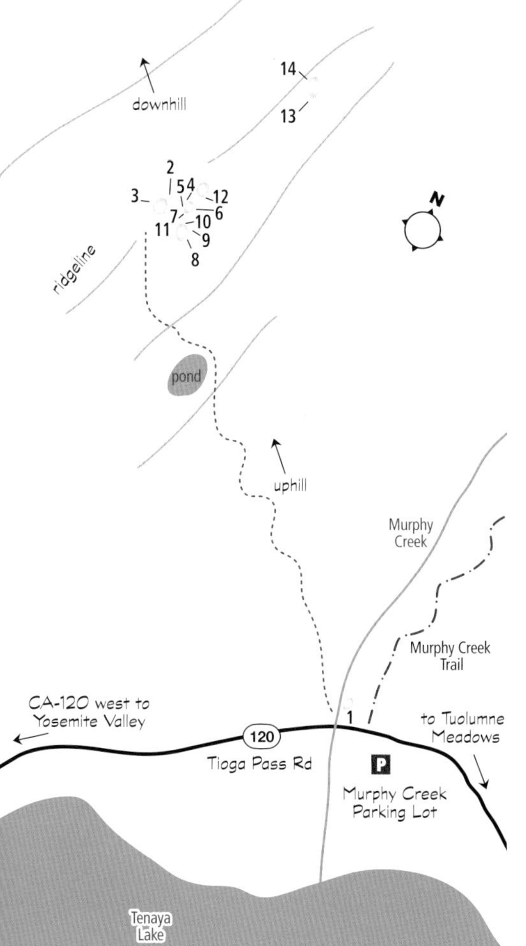

❑ **10. Booze Bottle V6★★★★** Stand start left of arête. Make moves up right around the "booze bottle" shaped arête. V9 Sit start. Mega classic! FA John Bachar 80's

❑ **11. V5R★★★** High dyke slab. FA Bachar.

Slash Boulder

❑ **12. V8★★★** Slash face. FA Charlie Barrett.

North Boulder

❑ **13. V1★★** Stand start the high arête!

❑ **14. V2★★** Stand start the high face!

❑ **15. V3★★** Sit start roof.

Tenaya Lake

Number of problems: **15 total/12 listed**

Time of Day: **All day Sun**

Difficulty: **VB-V?**

Tenaya Lake is an unmistakable landmark. With Stately Pleasure Dome standing tall and proud at its side and CA-120 slithering between them both, it marks the gateway to the rocky oasis ahead if coming from the west. On the far (southeast) side of the lake from the highway are a few boulders with a few good problems. On hot days the lake is also a nice place to take a dip or just hang out and have a picnic.

DIRECTIONS:

Park at the east end of Tenay Lake, which is about 7.4 miles west of the Tuolumne Meadows Store or 31.50 miles east of Crane Flat (about 2.7 miles east of Olmstead Point) Parking GPS: 37.83808, -119.45208

APPROACH:

Approach time ten minutes. From the bathrooms at the east end of Tenaya Lake, walk along the east shore to the southeast corner of lake where a hiking trail runs east/west. Right when you hit the main hiking trail, there is a ten-foot rounded boulder. Just left of this, a climber trail heads south up the hill toward Tenaya Peak. Walk on this for a few minutes/few hundred yards until the trail touches a six-foot tall boulder on the right and two-foot flat boulder on the left. Turn left (west), walk over a dead tree, and continue a few hundred feet east. You will see a few boulders, including the project boulder. The problem faces east. GPS of main boulder: 37.83320, -119.44931

❑ **1. V1★★** Jump start up right to arête.

❑ **2. V1★★** Arête.

❑ **3. V2★★** Thin slab.

❑ **4. V2★★** Start right-hand sidepull up to rail.

❑ **5. V2★★** Sit start (warm up for V8)?

❑ **6. V2/3★★** Sharp arête.

❑ **7. V1★★** Mantel.

❑ **8. V3/4★★** Left-hand sloper – right-hand edge – up past knob.

❑ **9. V1★★** Golden knobby edges.

❑ **10. V6★★** Arête.

❑ **11. V1★★** Shallow crack.

❑ **12. V8?★★** or V?? project? or??

Peter Croft bouldering near the base of Crescent Arch, Daff Dome. Photo by Chris Falkenstein

Number of problems by difficulty

VB	V0	V1	V2	V3	V4	V5	V6	V7	V8	V9	V10	≥V11
0	0	5	4	1	0	0	1	0	1	0	0	0

Tenaya West

Number of problems: **25 total/15 listed**

Time of Day: **Sun/Shade Mix**

Difficulty: **VB-V10**

Directly across from East Tenaya Lake are a few great boulders with a variety of angles and grades. The powerful Roadside Cave, the old school classic Kamps Boulder and all the boulders around them offer up enough quality problems for a good session on friction slabs and knob pinches! Just east of the Kamps Boulder/Roadside Cave area and just west of Tenaya East is the Texas Radio Boulder with a few notorious highballs and the fun Lunge.

Chris McNamara tunes into Texas Radio V3R

DIRECTIONS:

31.70 miles east of Crane Flat (about 2.9 miles east of Olmstead Point) + 26.70 miles west of Lee Vining/CA-395 (about 7.2 miles west of the Tuolumne Meadows Store) on Tioga Pass Rd./CA-120. Parking GPS: 37.83808, -119.45208

APPROACH:

Obvious boulders across the road from the East Tenaya Lake Parking Lot. All boulders are within a five-minute walk from the parking.

Kamps Boulder/Roadside Cave (L to R)

❑ **1. Kamps Boulder** V0-V2★★★ 4-5 good fun problems on a clean slab boulder.

❑ **2. V0★** Sit start. Go up over the left side.

❑ **3. V1/2★★** Same sit as V0 , then up right along arête to top.

❑ **4. Roadside Cave V5★★★** Stand start overhang or V10 low start undercling!

Number of problems by difficulty

VB	V0	V1	V2	V3	V4	V5	V6	V7	V8	V9	V10	≥V11
0	4	3	2	2	1	0	1	1	0	0	1	0

❑ **5. V0/1★★** Stand start arête – Sit V3/4

Roadside Rock

❑ **6. Roadside Roof V4R★★** Highball roof!

❑ **7. Steins Arête V2R★★** Highball arête/face!

❑ **8. V?**

Texas Radio Boulder (R to L)

❑ **9. Texas Radio V3R★★★** Classic highball right-hand arête/corner. Technical crux low. Mental crux up High! FA Dale Bard 80s.

❑ **10. White Glove V7R★★★** Highball left-hand arête! FA: Dean Potter 90s.

❑ **11. V1★★** Left arête.

❑ **12. The Lunge V3★★★** Stand start in center of NE face. Lunge or static to rail.

❑ **13. V2★★** Right slab start to The Lunge.

❑ **14. V1★★** Left side of (right-hand) arête.

❑ **15. V0★★** Right side of arête/slab – easy way to up/downclimb

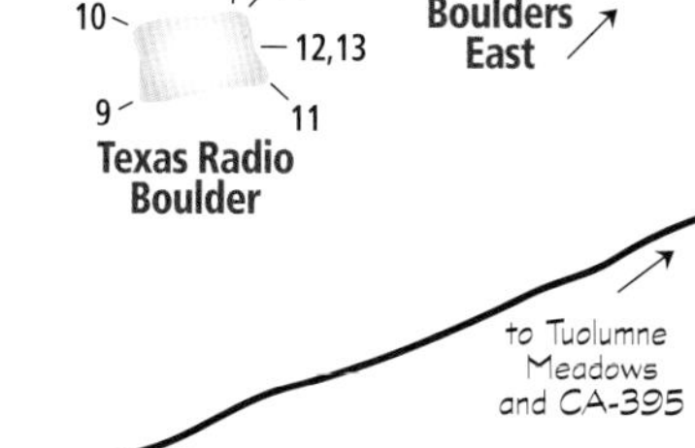

Tenaya East

Number of problems: **35 total/20 listed**

Time of Day: **Sun/Shade Mix - Mid Day Sun**

Difficulty: **V0–V8**

This is one of the best areas in Tuolumne with its huge granite blocks on smooth slabs off the side of the highway and the towering cliffs rising up from every side. It is not to be missed. One of the best problems greets you at the door — the perfect Reach For a Peach (V6) is solid for the grade and a proud send. There are also some great moderates like the classic semi-highball jug haul Flakes.

John Bachar on Reach For a Peach. Photo: John Bachar Collection

DIRECTIONS:

32.00 miles east of Crane Flat (about 3.1 miles east of Olmstead Point) + 26.40 miles west of Lee Vining/CA-395 (about 7.0 miles west of the Tuolumne Meadows Store) on Tioga Pass Rd./CA-120 The Cube GPS: 37.84010, -119.45090

APPROACH:

Obvious boulders on the hillsides and slabs above the northwest side of Tioga Pass Rd. (CA-120) about a five-minute walk northeast of the Tenaya West Boulders and just a one-to-two-minute hike uphill from the road.

Reach For a Peach Boulder (L to R)

❑ **0. Kamps Problem V1★★★** A classic old school face climb. Used to be the testpiece on the boulder back in the day (was rated 5.10c). FA Bob Kamps 70s.

❑ **1. Reach For a Peach V6★★★★** Stand start steep left-hand arête – V8 Low start. FA John Bachar 80s.

❑ **2. V2★★** Stand start around and right of Reach For a Peach.

The classic Flakes on The Cube.

❑ **3. V2★★** Stand start far right of Reach For a Peach.

Number of problems by difficulty

VB	V0	V1	V2	V3	V4	V5	V6	V7	V8	V9	V10	≥V11
1	3	4	8	2	2	0	1	0	1	0	0	0

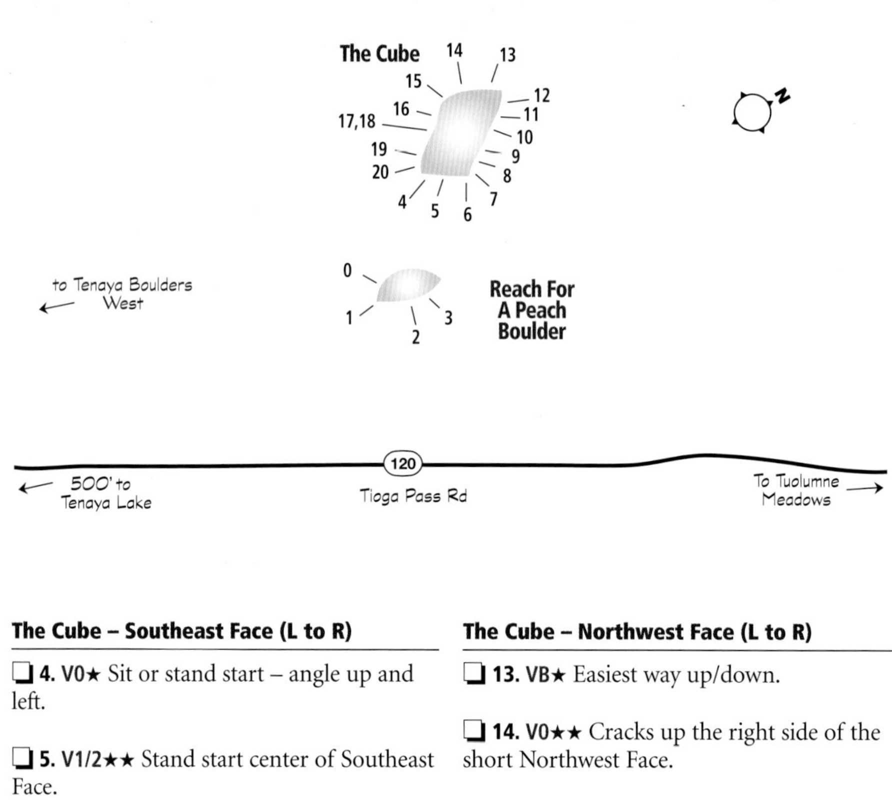

The Cube – Southeast Face (L to R)

❑ **4. V0★** Sit or stand start – angle up and left.

❑ **5. V1/2★★** Stand start center of Southeast Face.

❑ **6. The Cube V0★★★** Fun crack/arête.

The Cube – Northeast Face (L to R)

❑ **7. Flakes V1★★★★** Start on the arête and follow the jug flakes up the right side.

❑ **8. Crimpee Edges V3★★★** Stand start on the tiny namesake "crimper edges" – Sit V!?

❑ **9. Cube Face V2★★★** Reachy stand start up center of face past laybacks and gastons.

❑ **10. Kauk's Pebbles V4★★★** Face right of the center problem on pebble-size knobs.

❑ **11. V2★★** Low start on undercling – up rail, up left.

❑ **12. V2★★** Far right side of Northeast Face.

The Cube – Northwest Face (L to R)

❑ **13. VB★** Easiest way up/down.

❑ **14. V0★★** Cracks up the right side of the short Northwest Face.

The Cube – Southwest Face (L to R)

❑ **15. V1★★** Low start on undercling , then up left into V0 crack on northwest face.

❑ **16. V2★★** Same low start on undercling, then direct up right rails – V0 start on rock.

❑ **17. V2★★** Traverse undercling below mini roof up left into V1 finish.

❑ **18. V3★★** Traverse undercling below mini roof left into direct V2 finish.

❑ **19. V4★** Traverse from far right side of face over rocks into undercling traverse.

❑ **20. V2/3★★** Go up right side of face.

20
4
5
6

7
8
9
10
11
12

The Knobs

Number of problems: **100 total/55 listed**

Time of Day: **Sun/Shade Mix - Late Afternoon Shade**

Difficulty: **VB–V7/8**

When I first bouldered in Tuolumne 20 years ago The Knobs were the main place. It was even featured in the ultra classic climbing movie of the time, Masters of Stone. One of the original Yosemite Stonemasters, Ron Kauk did a rare (rare back then) dyno and even a double dyno just for fun. It was one of the most radical stunts I'd ever seen! Dynos were almost totally unheard of back in the late 1980s/ early 90s. The problem is easy to find in the list below, it's called Double Dyno and is actually more commonly done with two single dynos (which is still technically a double dyno) but to do a true double (two-handed) dyno on the big second dyno to the top lip is the super bonus party trick and sort of a goofy Knobs tradition. Named after the common Tuolumne hold, the Diorite Knob, this is the place to get your fingers used to pinching, crimping, and standing on the tiny grips. A high concentration of classic problems from VB to V-hard take mostly plumb lines up several blocks scattered around the forest. Most of the problems are above flat stone slabs and all are right off the road. It's no wonder that these are still some of the most popular boulders in Tuolumne. Here is a quote from one of the Yosemite Stonemasters, John Bachar, about the boulder problems at the Knobs:"I used to train on these things extensively to prepare for the Bachar Yerian and other Tuolumne first ascents. Especially the traverses. They are still difficult today."

The Author doing a lap on the Kauk Problem. Photo Adrian..

DIRECTIONS:

33.00 miles east of Crane Flat (about 3.9 miles east of Olmstead Point) + 25.40 miles west of Lee Vining/CA-395 (about 6.0 miles west of the Tuolumne Meadows Store) on Tioga Pass Rd./CA-120 Parking GPS 37.85231, -119.44105

APPROACH:

Obvious boulders scattered on the slabs and hillsides to the northwest of the parking alongside Tioga Pass Rd. (CA-120). All are within a five-minute walk of the road.

Number of problems by difficulty

VB	V0	V1	V2	V3	V4	V5	V6	V7	V8	V9	V10	≥V11
4	11	7	9	12	1	2	0	1	1	0	0	0

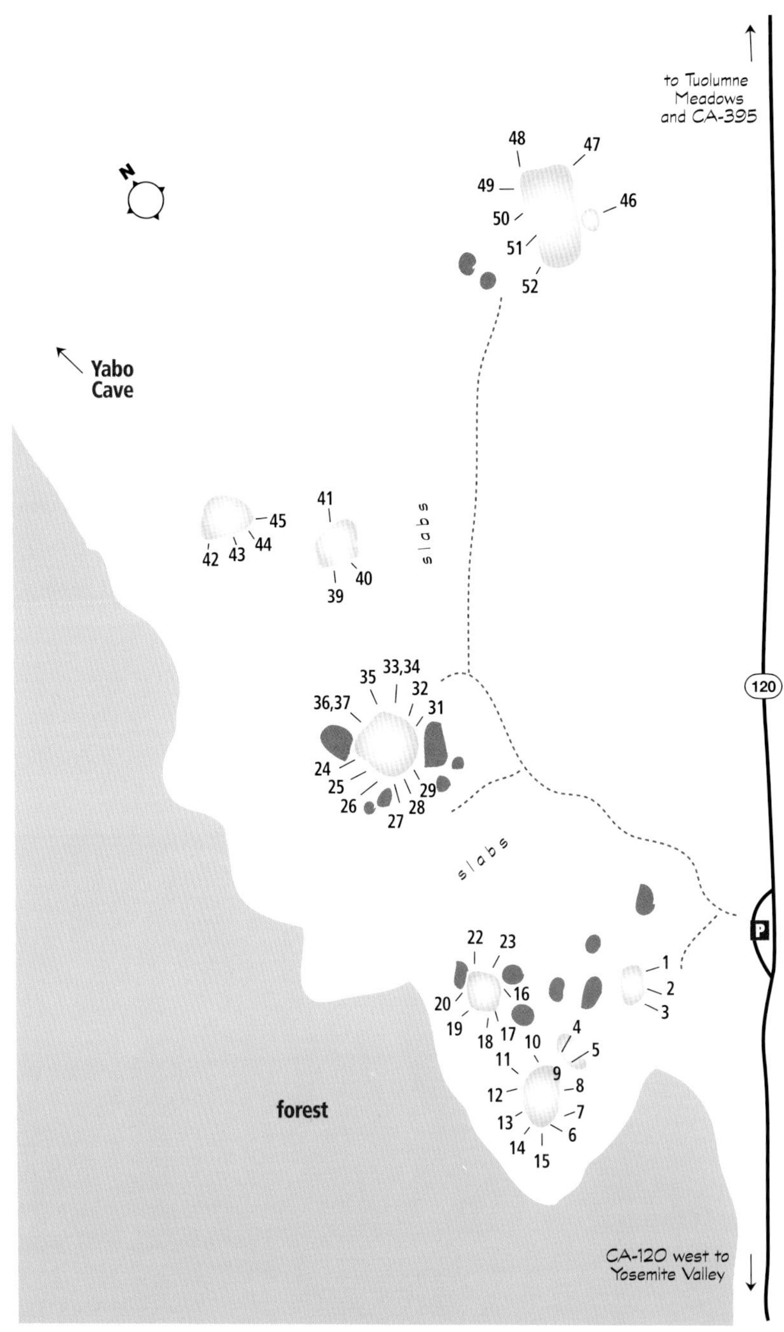

to Tuolumne Meadows and CA-395
N
Yabo Cave
48
47
49
46
50
51
52
41
45
44
42
43
40
39
slabs
35
33,34
32
36,37
31
24
25
29
26
28
27
120
slabs
P
22
23
1
16
2
20
3
19
18
17
10
4
11
5
9
8
12
7
13
6
14
15
forest
CA-120 west to Yosemite Valley

Forest Boulder (R to L)

❑ **1. V2★★** Sit start on sloper edge.

❑ **2. V2★★** Stand start on left-hand layback.

❑ **3. VB★★** Slab crack.

So Low

❑ **4. So Low Left V1★★** Low stand start matched on horizontal edge – one move to top.

❑ **5. So Low Right V2★★** Low sit start on low lip – low detached rock is on for feet. There is a traverse with mantle start right of 5. Traverse under roof, to jug left of 4 and mantle. FA Bard or Falkenstein.

Creek Boulder (L to R)

❑ **6. V2/3★★★** Shallow corner up steep slab face.

❑ **7. V1/2★★★** Knobby arête/corner.

❑ **8. V1★★★** Center of steep slab face.

❑ **9. Creek Arête V0★★★★** Either side Northeast arête – knobby, high, slab classic!

❑ **10. V1★★** Center of slab face to thin crack top out.

❑ **11. V0★★** Short, slopey and knobby, slab arête.

❑ **12. V3/4★★** Face right of arête and left of small tree.

❑ **13. V0★** Stand start short diagonal crack to dirty groove.

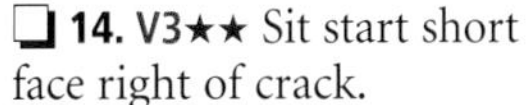

❑ **14. V3★★** Sit start short face right of crack.

❑ **15. V0★** Short arête.

Knob Boulder aka Big Boulder (R to L)

❑ **16. V3★★** Low sit start on short sloper right arête.

❑ **17. V1★★★** Same low start on prow as V0, then go up right along rail to jug top.

❑ **18. V0★★** Low start on good holds on prow and go up.

❑ **19. Knob Face V0★★★** Center of knobby slab face over flat slab rock landing.

❑ **20. VB★★** Slab next to rocks.

❑ **21. VB★★** Slab over rocks.

❑ **22. V0★★** Right arête.

❑ **23. V0★** Left arête.

Eliminator Boulder – West Face (L to R)

❑ **24. V0★** Knobby left arête.

❑ **25. V0★★** Center of knobby steep slab face from low horizontal crack start.

❑ **26. V0★★** Stand start prow.

Eliminator Boulder – South Face (L to R)

❑ **27. V1★★** Stand or sit right of prow then traverse right along jug rail/ledge into same top out as The Layback.

❑ **28. V3★★★** Center of golden knobby face left of Layback. or V3 Left or Right variations. V4 Sit start.

❑ **29. The Layback V2★★★** Right-hand layback rail on knob face over slab rock landing.

❑ **30. The Door Knob V3★★★** Stand start big knobby face right of Layback. V4 Sit start.

❑ **31. V5/6/7★★**

Eliminator Boulder – East Face (L to R)

❑ **32. The Hardest Problem at the Knobs V7/8★★★** Low start in corridor – go up right.

❑ **33. Kauk Problem V5★★★★** Stand start on horizontal crack/ rail left of Double Dyno and crimp and hook your way up to and over the knobby lip. V6 Sit start same as Double Dyno. FA Ron Kauk 80s.

❑ **34. Snake Eyes V2★★★★** Stand start same as Double Dyno, then bust a reachy move up left to "snake eye" knobs and crank past them to the top lip — V3 sit start same as Double Dyno. FA Chris Falkenstein 80s.

❑ **35. Double Dyno V2★★★★** Stand start on horizontal crack/rail and throw a big dyno move up right — V3 sit start and toss a short dyno up into the stand start for the true Double Dyno! FA Falkenstein 80s.

❑ **36. V1★★★** Stand start right of Double Dyno and pull over bulge.

❑ **37. V0★★★** Stand start on horizontal crack on right side of face with rock to the right and go up knobby face.

❑ **38. Eliminator Traverse V7★★★** SStart on right side of face same as V0 or on the rock on the right side and traverse horizontal crack left past Double Dyno and Snake Eyes into the Kauk Problem. FA John Bachar 80s..

John Bachar on Eliminator Center (28) c. 1980. Photo by Chris Falkenstein

BEAL

Mushroom – South Face

❑ **39.** V2★★ Sit start mini roof up knob face.

❑ **40.** V2★★ Sit start knobby roof bulge left of arête.

Mushroom – East Face

❑ **41.** V2★★ Left or right face.

Cross Boulder

❑ **42a.** V3★★★ Stand start steep knob face. Go up left.

❑ **42b.** V3★★★ Stand start steep knob face. Go up center.

❑ **42c.** V3★★★ Stand start steep knob face. Go up right.

❑ **43. The Cross** V3★★★ Left or right starts up knobby bulge.

❑ **44. Bachar Traverse** V5/6/7★★★

❑ **45.** VB★★ Slabby right side.

Liv Sansov burns a lap on the Kauk Problem.

The Scoop Boulder, Northeast Face (L to R)

❑ **46. V0R★** Easiest way up/down.

❑ **47. The Scoop V3★★★★** Sit start up past knobby scooped face to classic top out!

❑ **48. The Scoop Arête V2★★★** The right arête of The Scoop.

❑ **49. V2R★★** Up slab left of crack.

❑ **50. V1/2★★** Up slab to crack, then diagonal traverse right and up. Top out high.

❑ **51. V2★★** Stand start steep knobby slab just right of center to high crack top out.

❑ **52. V3/4★★** Stand start in small scoop and go up into high crack top out.

Yabo Cave 53-55 FA John Bachar 80's

(uphill northeast of the Cross Boulder)

❑ **53. Yabo Flake V3★★★** Flake in cave.

❑ **54. Bachar Problem V4★★★** Face in cave.

❑ **55. Cave Traverse V5/6/7★★★** Tough knobs!

Ron Kauk does the classic Scoop. Photo by Chris Falkenstein

Medlicott Boulder

Number of Problems: **25 total/12 listed**

Time of Day: **Shade All Day**

Difficulty: **VB-V7/8+**

A bit of forest wandering might be needed the first time you hike up to this giant block. But don't be discouraged, it's not very far or I would have not made it my lazy self. This is a massive rock, so once you find it you will not easily forget where it is. In fact I can hardly call it a boulder because it is more of a crag or small clifflet. There are problems on almost every side from VB to V-hard and a nice variety of highballs and semi-highballs with very few lowballs. Most of the problems are classic.

DIRECTIONS:

34.00 miles east of Crane Flat (about 4.9 miles east of Olmstead Point) + 24.40 miles west of Lee Vining/CA-395 (about 5.0 miles west of the Tuolumne Meadows Store) on Tioga Pass Rd./CA-120 Parking GPS: 37.86243, -119.43353

APPROACH:

This is a 5-10 minute approach. From the parking on the southeast side of Tioga Pass Rd. (CA-120) at the boggy meadow, follow the faint climber trail past the meadow to a hiker trail and take it to the left. After a few minutes, turn right onto a faint climber trail leading slightly uphill to the Medlicott Boulder. If you get lost, just walk toward the main cliff and find a high point that you can look down from. The main boulder is near the junction of a distinct talus field and the forest. Medlicott Boulder GPS 37.86291, -119.42940

Medlicott Boulder - South Face. Photo by Chris Falkenstein

Medlicott Boulder – South Face (L to R)

❑ **1. V3/4R★★★** Diagonal crack to high top out! FA John Bachar.

❑ **2. V?** Face??

❑ **3. V7/8★★★** Vertical seam to small knobs.

❑ **4. V6/7★★★** Crimper knob face.

❑ **5. V2/3★★** Arête.

Medlicott Boulder – East Face (L to R)

❑ **6. V4/5★★** Right of tree – start off tree?

❑ **7. V?** Crimper sit??

❑ **8. V?** Stand start next to tree?

❑ **9. VB★** Slabs.

Medlicott Boulder - North Face (L to R)

❑ **10. V1★★** Sit start short shady left arête to ledge – V0 stand start.

❑ **11. V4★★** Low stand start on blocky jug, then up left to finish on the arête – V5 sit.

❑ **12. V?** Direct face!

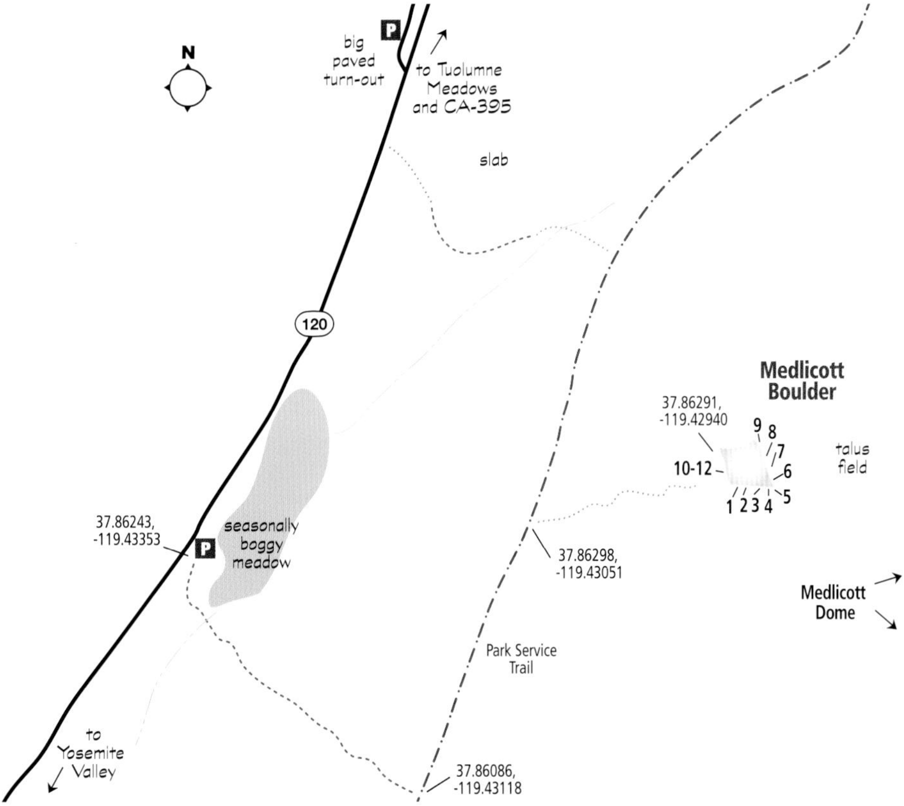

N
P
big paved turn-out
to Tuolumne Meadows and CA-395
slab
120
Medlicott Boulder
37.86291, -119.42940
9 8
7
6
5
10-12
1 2 3 4
talus field
37.86243, -119.43353
P
seasonally boggy meadow
37.86298, -119.43051
Medlicott Dome
Park Service Trail
to Yosemite Valley
37.86086, -119.43118

The Gunks

Number of Problems: **50 total/25 listed**

Time of Day: **Shade All Day - North Facing**

Difficulty: **VB-V10**

Reminiscent of the rocks at the Gunks in New York, with horizontal slashes and cracks, it's easy to see where it got the name. Discovered by John Bachar and Dave Yerian in the 1980s, this boulder-strewn cliff-band hosts many a classic line. On the left side of the main wall the epic Steelfingers Traverse is the obvious long, technical horizontal crack/face traverse. Rising above the traverse are the classics Cellulite Eliminator (V7) and Gunks Crack (V1). To the northwest of the main wall are a pile of good moderates and the fun problem known simply as The Arête (V4). A short hike up right (west) of the main wall will get you to the Mean Greens, a few good highballs and a cool traverse. For pure bouldering this is one of the best areas in Tuolumne, with fewer crowds, a short hike, and a nice selection of well-featured classics.

Liv Sansoz floats the Cellulite Eliminator.

DIRECTIONS:

36.30 miles east of Crane Flat (about 7.3 miles east of Olmstead Point) + 22.10 miles west of Lee Vining/CA-395 (about 2.6 miles west of the Tuolumne Meadows Store) on Tioga Pass Rd./CA-120. Parking GPS: 37.88121, -119.39908

APPROACH:

From the parking follow a small trail for two minutes uphill to the south. The bouldering is on the small cliff-band and the boulders that surround it. GPS of Boulders: 37.88070, -119.40008

1-25 FA John Bachar 1980's

Steelfingers Wall (L to R)

❑ **1. Steel Fingers Traverse V8★★★★**

Horizontal crack and face traverse – usually done from left to right starting at a no hands rest. V10 Low Variation:

Here is Bachar's Beta: "Steelfingers is old school 12c/d the high way (high left and then high right finish. It's probably 13a if you go low left and then low right. The traverse goes both ways and I used to do countless laps on this thing. I think the hardest way is starting far right and going low right to the low left (13a/b old school)"

Number of problems by difficulty

VB	V0	V1	V2	V3	V4	V5	V6	V7	V8	V9	V10	≥V11
0	4	7	5	0	3	0	1	2	2	0	1	0

❑ **2. V0R★★** Stand start on left side same as Steelfingers ,then go up high slabby face.

❑ **3. Cellulite Eliminator V7★★★★** Sit start under roof — V5 Stand start above roof.

❑ **4. V4★★★** Low sit start same as Cellulite Eliminator, then reverse the Steelfingers start.

❑ **5. Gunks Crack V1★★★★** Classic overhanging splitter crack from a sit or stand start!

❑ **6. V1★★** Face just to the right of the crack.

❑ **7. V0★★** Face climb up far right side of Steelfingers Wall.

Gunks Boulder (L to R)

❑ **8. V1★★** Left arête.

❑ **9. V2★★** Black and white face right of arête with horizontal slashes.

❑ **10. V2★★** Black and white center face with horizontal slashes.

❑ **11. V2/3★★** Right side of face.

❑ **12. V4★★** Traverse from low on the right side to the left along rail around arête.

Arête Boulder (L to R)

❑ **13. V0★★★** Stand start, then climb up and right around small roof.

❑ **14. V0★** Stand start on chunky left arête.

❑ **15. V1★★** Center of face with horizontal crack/slash holds.

❑ **16. V1R★★** Arête/slab over rocks.

❑ **17. V6★★** Traverse from left to right along horizontal crack around arête into The Arête – V5 from V1R arête start.

❑ **18. The Arête V4★★★** Sit start on jugs low in rocky crevice and climb up right along the steep, well-featured, white arête.

❑ **19. V4/5★★** Problem in tight rocky corridor.

The Mean Greens

❑ **20a. Mean Green Left V7/8★★★** Stand start left of steep green face.

❑ **20b. Mean Green Center V7/8★★★** Stand start left of steep green face.

❑ **21. Mean Green V8★★★** Low stand start right side of steep green face.

The Gunks – West

❑ **22. Pumpmaster Traverse V2/3★★★** Harder depending on where you start and finish. First ascentionist John Bachar: "We used to do laps there at the end of the session when we couldn't do the hard stuff to finish the pump off so to speak."

❑ **23. Reach For It, Left V1R★★** High face up left side. FA: John Bachar.

❑ **24. Reach For It, Right V1R★★** High face up center. FA: John Bachar.

❑ **25. V2/3R★★** High face up right side.

Cathedral Boulders

Number of Problems: **10+ total/1 listed**

Time of Day: **Sun/Shade Mix**

Difficulty: **V?-V4**

There is really only one well-known problem at the Cathedral Boulders: the splitter 20-foot roof crack known as Ghetto Snake (V4). But there are a lot of other random chunks and a lot of potential for exploration on the trails out to Cathedral Lake and Cathedral Peak.

DIRECTIONS:

Park on the side of Highway 120 at the Cathedral Lakes trailhead about 1.5 miles west from the Tuolumne Meadows Store.

APPROACH:

From the parking area at Cathedral Lake Trailhead, follow the popular Cathedral Lake Trail (past the left turn for the climbers trail to the base of Cathedral Peak) for about one mile from the road to a pile of large talus boulders on the left side of the trail. Ghetto Snake is a roof crack that splits the ceiling of a small cave in the pile of boulders.

Josh Holmes on Ghetto Snake. Photo by Chris Falkenstein.

Ghetto Snake Boulder

❑ **1. Ghetto Snake V4★★★** Splitter 20-foot roof crack only a few feet off the ground.

Chris Idiart on a random boulder near Cathedral Peak. Photo: James Hosler hoslerphotography.com

John Bachar on Mean Green 1980. Photo: John Bachar Collection

Puppy Boulders

Number of Problems: **50 total/30 listed**

Time of Day: **Sun/Shade Mix**

Difficulty: **VB-V12/13**

A cascading waterslide flows into a tranquil pool of water adjacent to these big boulders around the base of Puppy Dome's south face. Just a short walk from the huge parking lot down a nice trail is all it takes to get to the test-piece of the Tuolumne area, "Thunderbird" (V12/13) and many more classics at almost every grade in between. A few old and new school mantel test-pieces are also found here, along with the mega chill spot next to the river, which on a hot day is also a nice swimming hole.

DIRECTIONS:

39.70 miles east of Crane Flat + 18.70 miles west of Lee Vining/CA-395 on Tioga Pass Rd./CA-120 (0.8 miles east of Tuolumne Meadows store/gas station – take the road to the Tuolumne Lodge and take a right into the Wilderness Permit Parking Lot and park). Parking GPS: 37.87676, -119.34633

GPS Mantel Boulder: 37.874300, -119.34533

APPROACH:

From the southeast corner of the Wliderness Permit Parking Lot (behind the food storage boxes) follow the nice trail around the west side of Puppy Dome for about three to five minutes to the big boulders between Puppy Dome and the Tuolumne River.

Liv Sansoz does Excalibur Left by Twilight..

Puppy Dome – North Face

❑ **1. One Try Wall V2★★** Left - V1 Center - V1 Right

❑ **2. Machine World Traverse V3★★★★** Start on left side and traverse up and right.

Number of problems by difficulty

VB	V0	V1	V2	V3	V4	V5	V6	V7	V8	V9	V10	≥V11
2	6	5	2	7	2	0	1	1	0	0	1	0

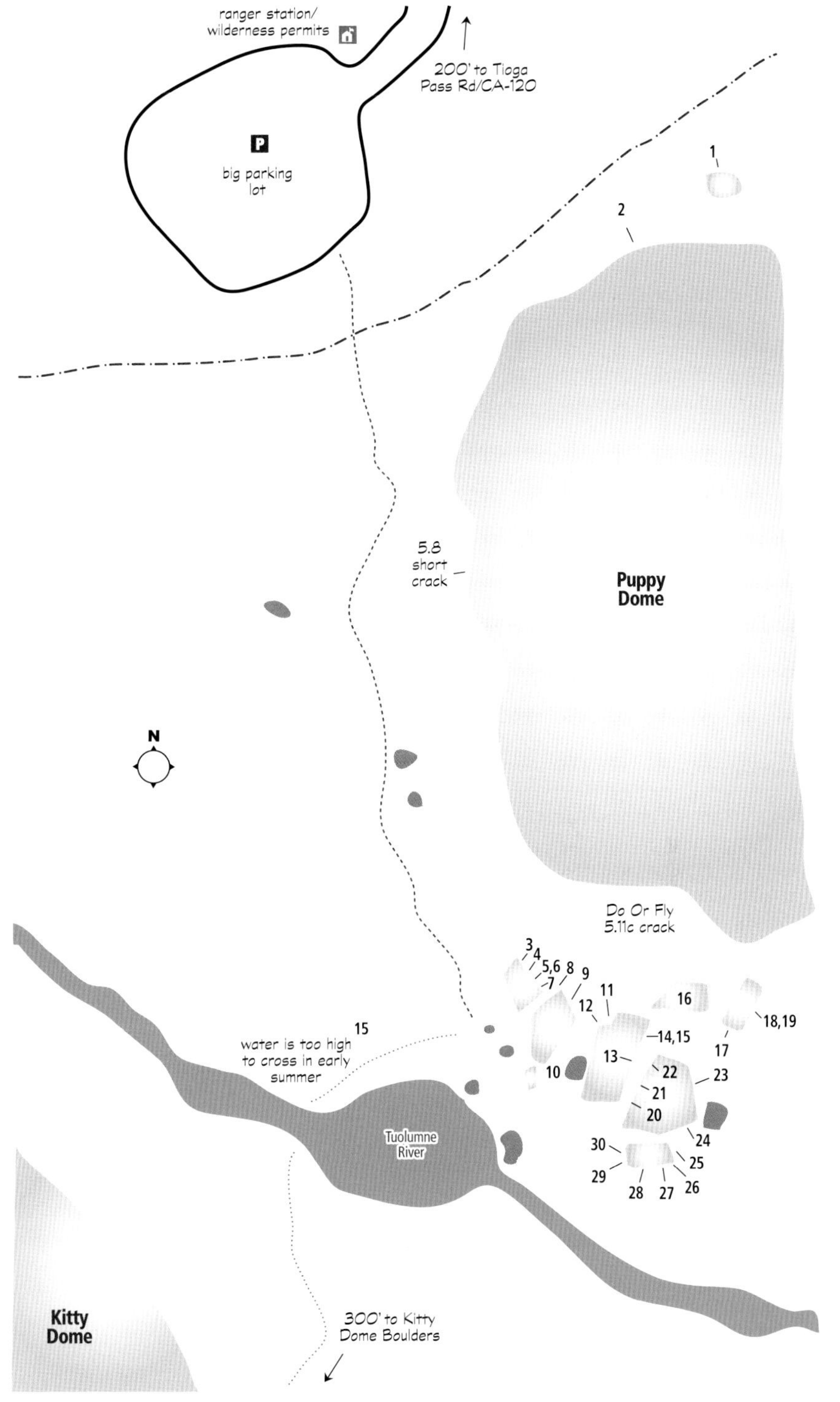
ranger station/
wilderness permits
200' to Tioga
Pass Rd/CA-120
big parking
lot
1
2
5.8
short
crack
Puppy
Dome
N
Do Or Fly
5.11c crack
3
4
5,6
7
8
9
11
12
16
18,19
14,15
17
13
22
23
21
20
10
24
25
26
27
28
29
30
15
water is too high
to cross in early
summer
Tuolumne
River
Kitty
Dome
300' to Kitty
Dome Boulders

Excalibur Boulder

❑ **3. VB★** Short right side of face.

❑ **4. Excalibur Right V3★★★** Right roof – low start.

❑ **5. Excalibur Left V3★★★** Left roof – low start.

❑ **6. Excalibur Traverse V3★★★** Traverse the roof in either direction – usually from right to left into Excalibur Arête.

❑ **7. Excalibur Arête V1★★** Low start then up left arête.

❑ **8. V0★** Stand start arête/ face on left boulder.

Ed's Eliminator Boulder

❑ **9. Ed's Eliminator V3★★★** Left, center or right. This technical face moves. Many pads.

❑ **10. V0★★** Traverse diagonal left-hand arête up and right to the top.

J.B.'s Boulder

❑ **11. J.B.'s Corner V4R★★★** Sit start on flat horizontal shelf in short dihedral – go up right into highball top out.

❑ **12. V4R★★** Traverse left and up into J.B.'S Corner – V5R sit start.

J.B.'s Boulder - The Gallery

❑ **13. The Gallery V0★★★★** Sit start on big edges and go up and left over lip. Or 13A: V2 lower lip traverse to same high top out as The Gallery.

❑ **14. V4★★★** Do low right/direct start to V0.

❑ **15. V2R★★** Upper right rail to high top out.

Wave Boulder

❑ **16. V1★★** Stand start on left boulder.

❑ **17. V1★★** Stand start left side of wave.

❑ **18. V0★★** Run and jump for the jug lip or stand start in the center of wave scoop!

❑ **19. V0★** Surf traverse the jug lip of the wave.

Mantel Boulder (R to L)

❑ **20. Sharma Mantel V7/8★★** Right mantel – new school sickness! FA Chris Sharma 90s.

❑ **21. Center Mantel V6/7★★** Center mantel – old school sickness!

❑ **22. Bachar Mantel V3★★★** Left mantel – old school classic. FA John Bachar 80s.

❑ **23. Thunderbird V12/13★★★★** Low start to steep, high, thin face test-piece! FA Chris Sharma 90s.

❑ **24. Ball Bearing V3★★** Stand start in horizontal crack, then face climb up left.

Cracked Boulder

❑ **25. VB★★** Slab crack or slab face right of crack.

❑ **26. V1★★** Arête – sit start.

❑ **27. V2/3★★** Stand start slab off rock.

❑ **28. V1/2★★** Stand start undercling – mantel top.

❑ **29. V0★★★** Slab crack.

❑ **30. V3★★** Slab face left of crack.

Kitty Boulders

Number of problems: **25 total/15 listed**

Time of Day: **Sun/Shade Mix - Afternoon Shade**

Difficulty: **VB-V7/8**

This is a secret local spot and if/when they find out it's in this book they are going to be pissed. So please, for both of our sakes hide this book when at the Kitty's. Don't even go unless you want to meet ornery locals and if you do go and get seen with the book by an ornery local just be nice and treat them like you would a bear and, most importantly, do not feed them.

Carlo Traversi on Golden Rastafarian. Photo by James Hosler.

Driving Directions/ Approach

Follow the same driving directions to the Puppy Boulders, then cross the Tuolumne River and hike over the hill on the east side of Kitty Dome to the boulders in a small nook. It's hard or impossible to cross the river in the early summer. GPS of boulder: 37.87248, -119.34693

Kitty Boulders - Main Area

❑ **1. V1★★★** Knobby arête – left start.

❑ **2. V2/3★★★** Knobby arête – direct/right start.

❑ **3. V7/8★★** Direct stand start variation – just right of arête.

❑ **4. V2★★★** Stand start knobby face right of arête – V4 Low start.

❑ **5. V1R★★** Slab prow.

Number of problems by difficulty

VB	V0	V1	V2	V3	V4	V5	V6	V7	V8	V9	V10	≥V11
0	0	6	6	1	1	0	1	1	0	0	0	0

❑ **6. V2/3★★** Overhanging prow. Or 6A: V2/3 Face right of prow Or 6B: V2/3 sloper right bulge.

❑ **7. V2★★★** Rail slab.

❑ **8. V4/5★★★** Left-handed arête start.

❑ **9. V1★★★** Right-handed arête start.

❑ **10. V1★★** Flake – downclimb.

❑ **11. V2★★** Slab arête – V3 sit start.

❑ **12. V1/2★★** Left or right start – or run and jump start.

Tombstone

❑ **13. Tombstone V2★★★★** Left arête.

Golden Rastafarian (L to R)

❑ **14. V1/2★★★** Stand start left arête , then up – or traverse right to top V2/3

❑ **15. Golden Rastafarian V3★★★★** AKA "The Guitar Problem" Stand start steep right-handed guitar shaped arête! – V6 sit.

Lee Vining Canyon

Number of problems: **35 total/25 listed**

Time of Day: **Sun/Shade Mix - Afternoon Shade**

Difficulty: **VB-V4+**

This is a nice place to boulder if it's cold up at high elevation and also a great place to camp for the same reason. With the Mobil only a few minutes away and usually plenty of campsites available to go with the fair amount of bulletproof granite in the canyon near the camping and the river, this is worth a visit for sure. The boulders have more edges, slopers, and square-cut holds rather than the knobby knobs so commonly found up in the Tuolumne area. There is some potential for new problems in the canyon and the problems that are already established are really good.

Lee Vining Canyon.

Driving directions:

54.5 miles east of Crane Flat (15.5 miles east of Tuolumne Meadows Store) + 3.5 miles west of Lee Vining/CA-395 on Tioga Pass Rd./CA-120 turn onto Poole Power Plant and , then turn right/west into Lee Vining Canyon. Follow separate directions to each area at the beginning of each section:

Roadside Boulder/Campground Boulder driving/approach

On Poole Power Plant Rd. about 0.3 miles from Tioga Pass Rd./CA-120. Parking GPS: 37.93021, -119.17115

There is no approach to the Roadside Boulder (obviously) and the Campground Boulder is visible in the forested campground less than a minute walk.

Number of problems by difficulty

VB	V0	V1	V2	V3	V4	V5	V6	V7	V8	V9	V10	≥V11
4	9	5	1	1	1	0	0	0	0	0	0	0

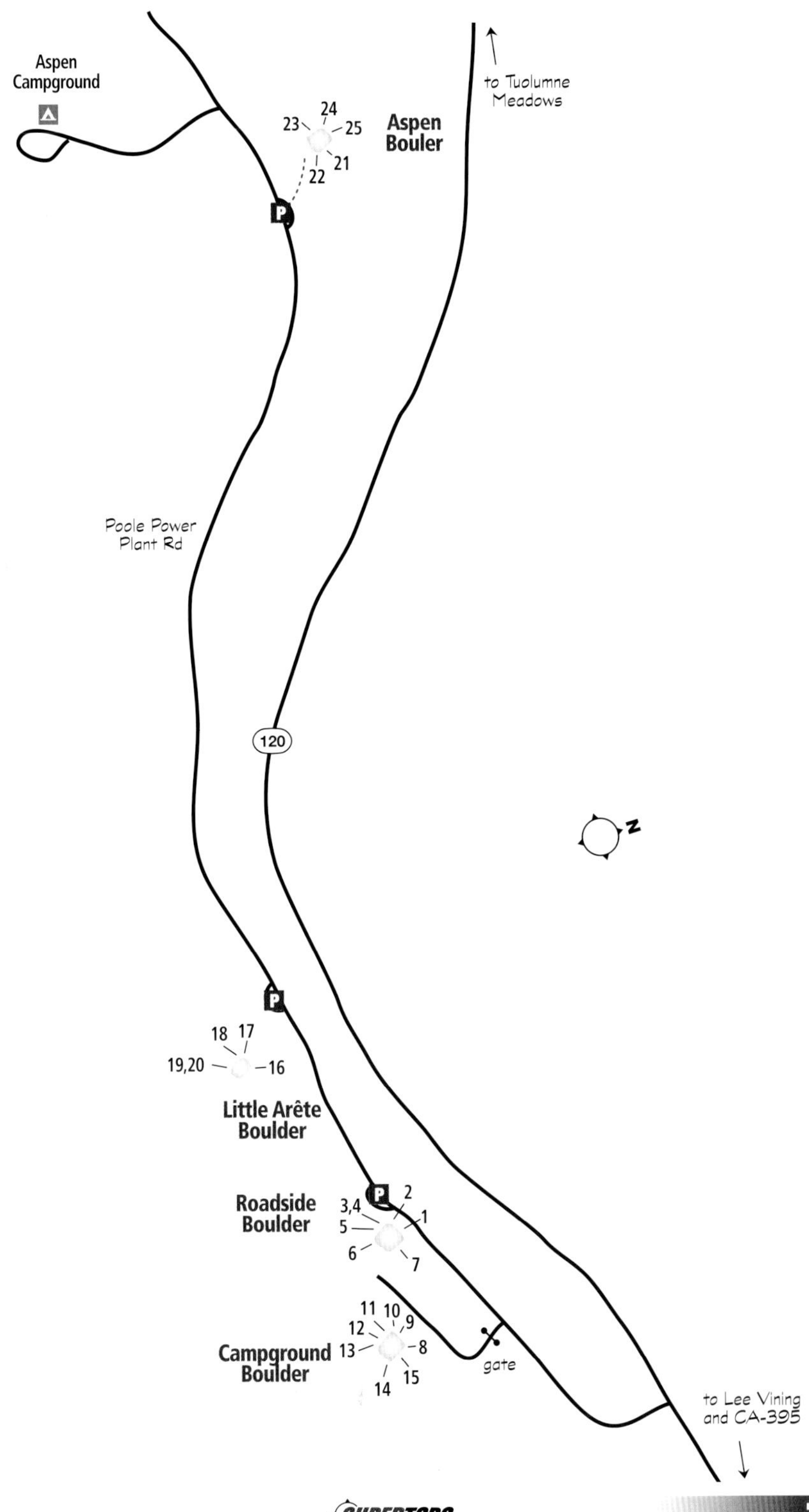
Aspen
Campground
24
23
25
Aspen
Bouler
21
22
to Tuolumne
Meadows
Poole Power
Plant Rd
120
18 17
19,20
16
Little Arête
Boulder
Roadside
Boulder
3,4
2
5
1
6
7
11 10
12
9
Campground
Boulder
13
8
14
15
gate
to Lee Vining
and CA-395

Roadside Boulder (left to right)

❑ **1. VB★** Slab face – up/downclimb.

❑ **2. V0★** Slab crack.

❑ **3. V3/4★★** Bulgey arête/prow.

❑ **4. Roadside Traverse V1★★★** Traverse from V0 slab crack start right past prow to end on V0 face.

❑ **5. Roadside Rails V0★★★** Face with big edge rails – top out up right.

❑ **6. V?** Arête project!?

❑ **7. V0★** Slab face.

Campground Boulder

(left to right 360 degrees around boulder - seen from trail as you approach)

❑ **8. V1/2★★** Left arête/face.

❑ **9. V1★★** Center face.

❑ **10. V0★★** Right arête/face.

❑ **11. VB★★** Left arête/slab.

❑ **12. V0★★** Slab face.

❑ **13. V1★★** Loose plate start.

❑ **14. V0★★** Stand start short prow – V2/3 Sit start low right-hand layback.

❑ **15. V?** Scoop/arête/face?

Little Arête Boulder driving/approach

On the left (creek) side of Poole Power Plant Rd. about 0.5 miles from Tioga Pass Rd./ CA-120. Parking GPS: N 37 55.853 W 119 10.451

Walk down the short embankment into the forest to the obvious Little Arête Boulder less than a minute from the road.

Little Arête Boulder (left to right)

❑ **16. VB★** Short bulge to slab.

❑ **17. V1★★** Right-hand slab/arête.

❑ **18. Little Arête V0★★** Left-hand arête/face with good rail edges.

❑ **19. V0★★** Stand start short right arête/ face – V1 Sit start.

❑ **20. V2★★** Slab/face traverse in either direction – delicate fun slab moves.

Aspen Boulder driving/approach

On the right (hill) side of Poole Power Plant Rd. about 1.3 miles from Tioga Pass Rd./ CA-120 just before and across from the entrance to Aspen Campground. Parking GPS: N 37 56.347, W 119 11.039

Walk uphill for less than a minute from the road past some birdhouses on the Aspen trees to the short but solid, multi-angled boulder.

Aspen Boulder (right to left)

❑ **21. V0★★** Slab face.

❑ **22. Aspen Arête VB★★★** Slab arête – easiest way to up/downclimb.

❑ **23. V1★★** Face rail start to mantel top.

❑ **24. V4★★★** Low stand start on sloper lumps or V? Sit?

❑ **25. V3★★★** Stand start matched on good rail or V? Sit?

5 Other Areas (A-E)

A-C May Lake

Number of Problems: Total: 50+
Time of Day: All day sun/shade mix

Potential to find new rock exists around the May Lake area, a lot of it being fairly obvious but some of it may take a little more exploration and imagination to discover. The three separate areas that are here may have only a few problems each but they are all high quality and totally worth the 20 to 30-minute hike. These areas are not just worth the hike for the quality of the rock but also for the pristine solitude, scenery, and possibility of discovery.

DIRECTIONS:

About 26.6 miles east of Crane Flat + About 31.8 miles west of Lee Vining/CA-395 (12.7 miles west of the Tuolumne Meadows Store) on Tioga Pass Rd/CA-120. Follow separate directions to the individual areas: Parking GPS: 37.83301, -119.49065

A. May Lake Cracks

APPROACH:

These two upside down splitter roof cracks are found in a small cave on the far west side of May Lake next to a small cove. Follow the trail from the parking lot up to May Lake and at May Lake Camp take a left and follow the trail around the lake to the west.

1 V2/3 Steep crack on left side of cave.

2 V4/5 Steep finger crack on right side of cave.

B. The Rock Slide

APPROACH:

This massive boulder pile/rock slide is on the same slabby, rocky hillside as The Tank. Follow the same approach as The Tank and hike down into the rock pile and choose a boulder and go at it! The Goldbug Boulder is in about the top/center of the pile.

3 Goldbugs Traverse V3 Traverse horizontal crack from right to left.

4 V? Highball face climbs – left, right or center of Goldbug Boulder?

C. The Tank

APPROACH:

This boulder can be a bit hard to find the first time. From the parking lot follow the main trail up to May Lake and at May Lake Camp take a right and hike around the east side of the lake. At about the end of the lake take a right off the trail and hike northeast up and over a slabby hillside to The Tank Boulder which is on the east aide of this slabby, rocky hill. Total hike time from parking lot is about 20 to 30 minutes.

5-10 V0-V?? A few uniquely featured, solid granite classics are found on this block.

D. The Drug Boulders

Not much is known about these boulders except that there are a few good problems already established here and potential for some more. There are also a few more boulders with possibilites around the base of the main face of Drug Dome below Oz.

DIRECTIONS:

Just to the west of Lamb Dome - About 34.5 miles east of Crane Flat + About 24.0 miles west of Lee Vining/CA395 (about 4.75 miles west of the Tuolumne Meadows Store) find parking in dirt pullouts on the side of Tioga Pass Rd/CA-120.

APPROACH:

Hike uphill on a small trail past the right (west) side of Lamb Dome toward Drug Dome which is obvious with the huge roof on top of its main face. After crossing a stream in the woods before Drug Dome head right (west) to the boulders below the right (west) side of Drug Dome.

Steve Schneider on The Flying Saucer Traverse, Cold Canyon. Photo by Chris Falkenstein

E. Cold Canyon

These are far out boulders that are far out on the north edge of the meadows near Tuolumne Falls. Some potential exists out here for a scouting boulderer with a love of the backcountry. With a night or more of supplies and a camping permit* who knows what kind of bouldering gems could be found in and around Cold Canyon and possibly all the way out to the northern edge of the park.

DIRECTIONS:

About 39 miles east of Crane Flat + About 19 miles west of Lee Vining/CA395 (about .02 miles west of the Tuolumne Meadows Store) on Tioga Pass Rd/CA120.

In Tuolumne Meadows from the parking areas at either the Glen Aulin Trailhead Parking Lot next to Lembert Dome or near the campground/store follow the main trails to the north side of the Tuolumne River. These trails all converge into the main Glen Aulin Trail that meanders northwest through the meadows toward Tuolumne Falls, Cold Canyon Boulders, and Glen Aulin High Sierra Camp. It is about a five-mile hike to Cold Canyon where you will find some established but as-of-yet uncharted boulder problems and potential for more. Also for about a .75 mile shortcut approach from Pothole Dome - ask a local/check a map for exact beta.

Other nearby climbing/bouldering areas

Don't miss the world class granite cliffs, walls, domes, and boulders in and around the Tuolumne and Yosemite Valley areas. [betabase.blogspot] The world renowned East Side of the Sierras along CA-395 has monolithic boulders of patina granite, solid volcanic tuff and a variety of other stone all within about a one to two-hour drive south of Tuolumne Meadows. [bishopbouldering.blogspot] Stretching from the Bachar Boulders, Clark Canyon and Deadman's Summit just south of Lee Vining to the areas around Mammoth like Way Lake and Pine Creek all the way down to the world class areas around Bishop like the Happy/Sad Boulders and the awesome Buttermilks are so many unimaginable boulder problems that they can fill all the days of the seasons but one – summer. Most of the East Side bouldering areas are too hot in summer. That's when Tuolumne takes over with its 9,000 foot elevations and high concentrations of granite boulderations!!

Other things to do

• Hot Springs! Near Mammoth, Bridgeport and Bishop. Ask a local or read a book then take a look and take a dip.
• Hiking in Tuolumne Meadows – Mt Dana, Cathedral Lake Trail, Glen Aulin Trail, May Lake Trail.
• Fishing – Lee Vining Canyon and all around Tuolumne Meadows and CA-395 from Reno to Bishop (about 30 minutes to 2 hours from Tuolumne Meadows)
• Sightseeing – The Tufa Formations at Mono Lake (30 minutes east of Tuolumne Meadows) near Lee Vining.

Chris Van Leuven on Mean Green. Photo by Chris Falkenstein

Mono Lake Tufa. Photo by James Hosler

5.10

Index

50 Suggested Classics

[In order they appear in book - west to east]

MORE FROM SUPERTOPO

LAKE TAHOE BOULDERING

$29.95 Available at www.supertopo.com

Lake Tahoe is quickly becoming California's largest summer bouldering area. There are more than 35 areas with more than 1,400 problems and new challenges are discovered every week. What sets Tahoe apart is not just the numbers, it is the variety. Climb Joshua Tree style rock by the lake or climb Yosemite-esque holds in the forest or drive 30 minutes east to the desert and climb impeccable volcanic pockets. It is all here, it is all year-round, and even this book, offering the most complete coverage yet on the subject, can only whet your appetite.

YOSEMITE VALLEY BOULDERING

$27.95 Available at www.supertopo.com

Yosemite Valley is one of the best granite bouldering areas in the world. This guide aims to inspire current and future Yosemite boulderers and makes Valley bouldering more accessible through clear descriptions, detailed topos, and numerous photos. This book includes many new problems and even completely new areas. From Camp 4 holdless desperates to classic moderates in serene settings, you will find the problems to suit your mood and motivation.

YOSEMITE VALLEY FREE CLIMBS

$29.95 Available at www.supertopo.com

This guidebook includes over 230 of the best routes in Yosemite Valley, from 16-pitch trad climbs to one-pitch sport routes. While many hard Yosemite test-pieces are included, this book focuses on topropes, crags, and multi-pitch climbs in the 5.4-5.9 range. We also include formerly obscure climbs to provide more options for avoiding crowds. As in all SuperTopo books, the authors personally climbed and documented each route with meticulous care to create the most detailed and accurate topos ever published.

MORE FROM SUPERTOPO

YOSEMITE BIG WALLS -2nd Edition

$29.95 Available at www.supertopo.com

Written by Chris McNamara, who personally climbed and painstakingly documented every route, this book includes essential route details such as climbing strategy, retreat information, descent topos, pitch lengths, and gear recommendations for each pitch. Yosemite Big Walls covers the 41 best big wall routes on El Capitan, Half Dome, Washington Column, and Leaning Tower.

TUOLUMNE FREE CLIMBS

$24.95 Available at www.supertopo.com

Tuolumne Free Climbs includes over 110 of the best routes in Tuolumne Meadows, from 14-pitch trad climbs to one-pitch sport routes. This book focuses on topropes, crags, and multi-pitch climbs in the 5.4-5.9 range. Includes formerly obscure climbs to provide more options for avoiding crowds. As in all SuperTopo books, the authors personally climbed and documented each climb with meticulous care to create the most detailed and accurate topos ever published.

HIGH SIERRA CLIMBING

$24.95 Available at www.supertopo.com

This guidebook includes 26 of the best High Sierra alpine climbs, ranging in difficulty from 3rd class to 5.11c. Most of these climbs are well-protected, 10 to 15 pitches long, and ascend some of the best alpine granite anywhere. Whether you plan to scramble up the 3rd class East Ridge of Mt. Russell, climb the 5.7 East Face of Mt. Whitney, or ascend the epic 18-pitch Sun Ribbon Arête, our guidebook ensures you spend minimum time getting off-route and maximum time enjoying the climbing.

About The Author

Chris Summit (yes it's his real name), was born to climb. A Northern California native, he started climbing and bouldering on the rocks around his home in Sonoma County where he grew up and still lives today. Since then his natural desire has evolved into a passionate obsession, changing his life forever for the better. In his 20 years of climbing Chris has written several guidebooks, including Bay Area and Northern California Bouldering by SuperTopo, and has worked at the North Bay's best climbing gyms setting routes, belaying, and teaching indoors and out. He has done first ascents of sport climbs, traditional climbs, and many boulder problems all over Northern California and has loved bouldering in Tuolumne ever since he crimped his first knob.

The author at The Knobs in the early 1990's
Photos (and inspiration!): Jason Coraza

MORE BY CHRIS SUMMIT

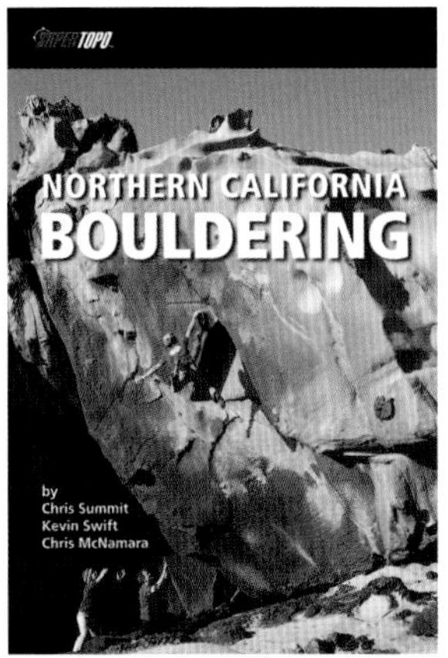

NORTHERN CALIFORNIA BOULDERING

$26.95 Available at www.supertopo.com

Northern California Bouldering highlights 50 of the best bouldering areas from just north of Yosemite all the way up to the Oregon border and west to the Pacific Ocean. With color maps, action photos and supertopo photos as well as detailed descriptions of all the boulder problems it's easy to use and easy on the eyes. Nearly every type of rock imaginable is included from limestone and sandstone to granite and volcanic tuff. All of the areas included are immersed in a variety of world class scenery from sea level to the alpine environments of the high Sierras.

BAY AREA BOULDERING

$24.95 Available at www.supertopo.com

Bay Area Bouldering includes over 700 boulder problems within a 2 hour drive of San Francisco. All the classic spots are in this book: Castle Rock, Indian Rock and Mickey's Beach, as well as a number of lesser-known spots on the North Coast. Sandstone, Schist, Rhyolite, Basalt and Chert are the most prevalent types of stone and each offers a very unique experience. This book includes everything from cruiser jug hauls on sandy beaches to sloper wrestling in lush forests. Author Chris Summit personally climbed and mapped almost every route to ensure the accuracy of the information.